TOTAL YOUTH MINISTRY

MINISTRY RESOURCES FOR

Justice and Service

Community Life

Youth Leadership Development

Pastoral Care

Prayer and Worship

Evangelization

To my family, for teaching me all I needed to know about being loved and accepted; to the parish community of Saint Vincent de Paul, for teaching me at such an early age that Church is the people of God; and to the good people of Saint Joseph University Parish, who play and pray together with such joy. Finally, this book is dedicated to all the communities I have had the pleasure of belonging to, the formal ones (Search and CLI teams, Confirmation Jubilee team, and Called to Witness) and the informal ones (Girls' Night Out, RAM, and card parties).

TOTAL YOUTH MINISTRY

MINISTRY RESOURCES FOR

Justice and Service

Community Life

Youth Leadership Development

Pastoral Care

Prayer and Worship

Evangelization

Ann Marie Eckert
Saint Mary's Press, Winona, Minnesota

Genuine recycled paper with 10% post-consumer waste.
Printed with soy-based ink. 5055601

Contributors
The following authors contributed to this manual:
Brenda Cline, Milwaukee, WI: "Who Am I?," "Making Friends," and "Music and Me"
Barbara Gawlik, Waterford, WI: "All Are Welcome"
Sean Lansing, Milwaukee, WI: "Catholic and American"
Debbie Olla, Brookfield, WI: "Let's Get Started" and "Sharing Our Faith: An Ecumenical Event"

Many people contributed to this resource with ideas, programs, and activities. Their contributions make this resource what it is. They are:
Kathie Amidei, Pewaukee, WI
Susie Dotson, Omaha, NE
Kathy Ebner, Camden, NJ
Carol Fischer, Greenfield, WI
Barbara Gawlik, Waterford, WI
Jenni Oliva, Milwaukee, WI
Debbie Olla, Brookfield, WI
Mary Osep, Milwaukee, WI
Brian Singer-Towns, Winona, MN
Eileen Warner, Buffalo, NY
Additional thanks to the youth ministry community in Milwaukee for their help in conceiving the contents of this resource.

The publishing team included Barbara Murray and Laurie Delgatto, development editors; Laurie Berg-Shaner, copy editor; Barbara Bartelson, production editor; Cären Yang, art director and designer; Jonathan Thomas Goebel, cover designer and pages 122–123 illustrator; Digital Images © PhotoDisc, Inc., cover images; Alan S. Hanson, pre-press specialist; Elly Poppe, CD-ROM developer; manufacturing coordinated by the production services department of Saint Mary's Press.

Produced with the assistance of settingPace, LLC, Cincinnati, Ohio.

Ministry resource manuals were developed in collaboration with the Center for Ministry Development. The publishing team included Thomas East, project coordinator, and Cheryl Tholcke, content editor.

Copyright © 2004 by Saint Mary's Press, Christian Brothers Publications, 702 Terrace Heights, Winona, MN 55987-1318, www.smp.org. All rights reserved. Permission is granted to reproduce only the materials intended for distribution to the program participants. No other part of this book may be reproduced by any means without the written permission of the publisher.

Printed in the United States of America

Printing: 9 8 7 6 5 4 3 2 1

Year: 2012 11 10 09 08 07 06 05 04

ISBN 0-88489-771-0

Contents

Introduction 7

Part A: Introductory Article

1 Community Is Essential to Youth Ministry 21

Part B: Community Life Sessions

2 Let's Get Started 27

3 Who Am I? 38

4 The Importance of Community 52

5 Making Friends 64

6 Music and Me 73

7 All Are Welcome 84

8 Trust 95

9 Catholic and American 105

10 The Changing Face of Friendship   113

Part C: Extended Program

11 Sharing Our Faith: An Ecumenical Event   127

Part D: Community-Building Strategies

12 Creating Community   141

13 Seasonal Suggestions for Community Building   149

14 Connecting Youth and the Parish   156

15 Peer Mentors for New Members:
Guardian Angel Program (GAP)   162

16 Promoting Positive Behavior in Community   168

17 Making the Most of Extended Events   175

18 Atmosphere, Attitude, and Actions   179

19 Helping Families Connect   183

Acknowledgments   187

Introduction

About Total Youth Ministry

Many youth today are waiting to hear the Good News that is ours as Christ's disciples. Youth in our parishes long to grow spiritually and to belong to their family, Church, and local community in meaningful ways. Parents of youth long to experience Church as supportive of and caring about the same things they care about. They hope the parish will offer ways for youth to be involved and to grow in their faith. Parents want to understand youth ministry so they can support and encourage their child's participation.

Parishes want to know how to include youth and how to pass on faith to a new generation. Parish members want to see youth more involved, and are worried about the challenges that face today's youth. They know that young people need support from their faith community—now more than ever. Parish youth ministry leaders are generous, passionate, and busy people; they make sacrifices so that youth will have a community to belong to and a place to grow. They need ideas and plans for youth ministry activities—and strategies that really work. They are working toward a ministry that goes beyond just gathering groups of young people; they are working toward a ministry that makes connections between youth and the community.

All those voices have something in common—a longing for youth ministry that is inclusive, dynamic, and flexible.

In 1997 the United States Conference of Catholic Bishops (USCCB) published its blueprint for youth ministry in the twenty-first century. *Renewing the Vision: A Framework for Catholic Youth Ministry* challenges youth ministry to focus its efforts in these directions:
- to empower young people to live as disciples of Jesus Christ in our world today
- to draw young people to responsible participation in the life, mission, and work of the Catholic faith community
- to foster the total personal and spiritual growth of each young person

In *Renewing the Vision*, the bishops urge the Church to guide young people toward a life of fullness in Jesus Christ, and to give them the tools that will enable them to live out that fullness as Catholic Christians. To put it simply, the bishops call young people to embrace their faith as they study it, pray it, and live it. The bishops also challenge the faith community to surround young people with love, care, and attention and to include youth throughout the life of the parish.

The Ministry Resource Manuals

The ministry resource manuals of the Total Youth Ministry series address each of the components of youth ministry as outlined in *Renewing the Vision*. The advocacy and catechesis components are woven throughout the ministry resource manuals. You will find the following information in each of the ministry resource manuals:

- a chapter explaining the component, connecting it to Church documents, and identifying practical ideas and resources for implementing the component
- sessions that can stand alone or be combined with others in the series
- numerous strategies, ideas, suggestions, and resources that go beyond a specific gathering

Following is a brief description of each of the manuals:

- *Ministry Resources for Community Life* offers faith communities program resources and strategies to build community among young people and throughout the entire parish. The resource includes nine gathered sessions to help young people get to know one another, themselves, and the meaning of Christian community. It also contains an outline for an ecumenical event to help build community across denominational lines, and it offers practical strategies and ideas to help manage community issues, make the most of community life opportunities, and encourage intergenerational and family relationships.
- *Ministry Resources for Evangelization* offers faith communities tools and program resources to evangelize youth. It offers practical strategies and ideas for outreach to young people and contains twelve gathered sessions to share the Good News. It also includes a retreat to engage young people in becoming or continuing as Jesus' disciples.
- *Ministry Resources for Justice and Service* offers faith communities programs and strategies to engage youth in justice, direct service, and advocacy in faithful, age-appropriate, and proactive ways. This resource contains eight gathered sessions around specific justice issues, an overnight retreat on service to poor people, and two half-day retreats or evening reflections on simplicity and racism.

- At the heart of *Ministry Resources for Pastoral Care* are twelve sessions designed to equip young people with the tools needed to celebrate their holy goodness and navigate some of life's difficult issues. The topics of the sessions include recognizing the goodness in oneself and others, building and maintaining relationships, dealing with tough times, and preparing for the future. The last section of the manual comprises strategies for doing the ongoing work of pastoral care.
- *Ministry Resources for Prayer and Worship* is designed for those who work with and walk with youth in this journey of discipleship. The manual contains three sessions to teach youth to pray and to practice praying in different forms. Eleven communal prayer services are included, which can be used on a variety of occasions throughout the seasons of the year. The manual also contains strategies and resources to help youth communities develop patterns of prayer and to include youth in preparing prayers and liturgies.
- *Ministry Resources for Youth Leadership Development* offers faith communities program resources and strategies to develop youth as leaders within youth ministry programs and the parish. The manual includes four foundational sessions on Christian leadership, ten leadership skill sessions and minisessions, and two sessions to help prepare youth and adults for working together. The manual offers ideas and strategies for creating leadership roles within the parish, inviting youth to leadership, and working with the parents of youth leaders. The plans for implementing sessions and other gathered events are complete, easy to follow, and adaptable to your community.

With the detailed plans provided for the sessions, activities, and strategies in Total Youth Ministry, youth ministry volunteers no longer need to be program designers. By using the Total Youth Ministry resources, you can focus on the important task of finding the leaders who make youth ministry happen. Each session includes an overview, a list of materials, preparation steps, and step-by-step instructions for facilitating a session with confidence. Most sessions also include a variety of ways to extend the theme of the session with prayer, related learning exercises, or follow-through experiences.

An Added Feature: CD-ROMs

Each manual has a CD-ROM that includes the full content of the manual. This feature enables the user to provide handouts and resource materials to adult leaders, parents, and the young people in a variety of delivery methods, such as e-mail, Web site posting, and photocopying. Handouts and resources are provided in printable color versions (which cannot be customized) and in black-and-white versions that you can customize for the particular needs of a group. You will also find hyperlinks to suggested Web sites.

Participant Resources

Much of the material in the ministry resource manuals is designed to work in a complementary way with the contents of *The Catholic Faith Handbook for Youth (CFH)* and *The Catholic Youth Bible (CYB)*.

Ministry Resources for Community Life: An Overview

Ministry Resources for Community Life offers faith communities program resources and strategies to build community among young people and throughout the entire parish. The resource contains nine gathered sessions to help young people get to know one another, themselves, and the meaning of Christian community. It also contains an outline for an ecumenical event to help build community across denominational lines, and it offers practical strategies and ideas to help manage community issues, make the most of community life opportunities, and encourage intergenerational and family relationships.

Manual Contents: An Overview

Part A: Community Is Essential to Youth Ministry

Chapter 1 of *Ministry Resources for Community Life* explores the importance of creating Christian community among youth and adults within the parish and the youth ministry program. It highlights the importance of creating an atmosphere in which youth are welcomed and an attitude of acceptance, as well as the importance of intergenerational relationships and the essential role the parish community plays in passing on faith.

Part B: Community Life Sessions

The community life sessions include opportunities for young people to learn more about themselves and other participants and to explore the Scriptures and our faith Tradition for images of Christian community. The sessions in this manual are about 60 minutes in length and sometimes include 15- to 30-minute session extensions. The sessions are not sequential, so you may organize them in the way that is most appropriate for your situation.

Each session begins with a brief overview, a list of expected outcomes, and background reading that may include a list of scriptural connections and *Catholic Youth Bible* article connections. All articles are excerpted from the first edition of the *CYB*. The next element is a suggested schedule, which is to be used as a starting point and modified according to your circumstances. A checklist of the preparation required, including all materials needed, is the next part of the presentation of every session. A complete description of the session procedure is then provided, including all activities, session extensions, prayer experiences, and options and actions.

Study It

Each session can be expanded and customized to meet your schedule and the needs of your group. You may expand the sessions by using additional activities known as session extensions. Musical selections from *Spirit & Song* are provided for your reference as well. A Bible concordance will provide additional citations if you want to add a more substantial scriptural component to a session, and music resources are available from a variety of publishers. Some of the sessions provide a list of media resources—such as print, video, and Internet—for more exploration. Family approaches provide simple, follow-up suggestions for family learning, enrichment, celebration, prayer, and service.

Pray It: Prayer Experiences

Each session includes opportunities and suggestions for prayer focused on the session's theme. Prayer forms include guided meditation, shared prayer, music, silence, prayer by young people, reflective reading, and experiences created by the participants. The Pray It component gives the young people an opportunity to bring their insights and concerns to God in prayer. The time frame for prayer experiences varies from 5 to 20 minutes.

Live It: Options and Actions

This manual can be a springboard for connections with other youth ministry experiences. Therefore most of its sessions include additional strategies to support the learning process. Those activities can be used to extend the session, provide good follow-up for the Study It core sessions, and allow for age-appropriate assimilation of the material.

Session Overviews

Chapter 2: Let's Get Started

- This session can be used at the beginning of a program year, at the start of a retreat, in preparation for a mission trip, or at any other time and place where helping people to know and trust one another is important. It is designed for participants who do not know one another, although it can be easily adapted for use with groups who are more familiar.

Chapter 3: Who Am I?

- In this session the participants are invited to use their gifts and talents to contribute positively to the communities in which they are involved, including their school, their local community, their parish, and the Church as a whole.

Chapter 4: The Importance of Community
- This session invites the participants to examine the importance of Christian community and the ways they are called to establish and participate in community.

Chapter 5: Making Friends
- This session helps young people take a closer look at the friends they have, the friends they are seeking, and the type of friend they wish to be.

Chapter 6: Music and Me
- In this session the participants experience different styles of music and recognize that music can help to celebrate the differences among people.

Chapter 7: All Are Welcome
- This session helps the participants recognize the need to include others and to be welcoming and open to everyone who participates in youth ministry programs.

Chapter 8: Trust
- This session is designed for groups that know each other but that may not currently be sharing at a deep level. The participants will be encouraged to think about the ways in which trust enhances relationships.

Chapter 9: Catholic and American
- In this session the participants look at the responsibilities of being Catholic and American, and how the Church challenges us to participate in our local community to make it a better place to live.

Chapter 10: The Changing Face of Friendship
- This session is intended for juniors and seniors in high school, to help them deal with the changes in friendships that may occur as they leave high school and move into college, the military, or a job setting.

Part C: Sharing Our Faith: An Ecumenical Event

Chapter 11 provides the framework for creating a 4-hour event to help young people of different faiths work together on service projects, express their belief in God creatively, and learn more about the different faith traditions. This event can be done as an ecumenical event, with young people from Christian faith traditions or from other faith traditions.

Part D: Community-Building Strategies

The strategies in part D of this manual offer parish leaders an opportunity to learn more about some of the components of community life within parishes. Many of these strategies will serve as excellent resources for youth ministry leaders to read and discuss. Parish leaders can examine their programs and events to look for ways to make the parish more youth friendly. Parents will benefit from lists of ideas for enhancing parent and teen relationships at home. Each strategy contains information to help leaders grow in their understanding of the issue, followed by practical strategies that can be implemented within the parish.

Strategies Overview

Chapter 12: Creating Community

- The essay included in this chapter provides an overview of the steps needed to develop community among all the participants of a youth ministry program or event. This chapter also provides an outline for leaders to follow when planning for and developing community-building events. You will also find a checklist to use when selecting community-building activities from other sources, as well as some simple guidelines for leading community-building activities.

Chapter 13: Seasonal Suggestions for Community Building

- This chapter contains a list of strategies and opportunities that can be used to create various youth ministry or parish initiatives. Program ideas and strategies for providing nongathered community building are included as well. These ideas help parishes celebrate the community that is already present and build community in new ways. In addition, they challenge participants to greater involvement in the wider local community.

Chapter 14: Connecting Youth and the Parish

- In this chapter you will find ways that leaders can be attentive to integrating youth within parish life and welcoming youth to parish events. Ideas for sponsored events to help the generations know each other better are included.

Chapter 15: Peer Mentors for New Members:
Guardian Angel Program (GAP)

- The Guardian Angel Program (GAP) encourages ninth-grade youth to participate in the parish youth ministry program. GAP provides an opportunity for welcome and outreach to those who are just starting high school, and supports their participation in a high-school-level youth ministry program.

Chapter 16: Promoting Positive Behavior in Community

- The strategies listed here assist youth ministry leaders in creating healthy groups and ensuring the safety—physical, spiritual, and emotional—of the young people in their care. To use these strategies successfully, all adults who work in the youth ministry program need to have a common understanding of the ways in which positive behavior can be promoted.

Chapter 17: Making the Most of Extended Events
- This chapter explores the ways in which retreats, mission trips, overnight service programs, and other extended-day events provide excellent opportunities for community building.

Chapter 18: Atmosphere, Attitude, and Actions
- Parishes can be attentive to community issues in countless ways. From setting up rooms to publicity to the use of music, simple details can make a big difference in the life of a community. These strategies will help any parish develop their own sense of community.

Chapter 19: Helping Families Connect
- This chapter addresses the common difficulties parents and their teenagers may face in communicating or spending quality time together, and offers hope that family ties can be enhanced and lived out in the adolescent years. It also contains specific ideas for things that families can do at home to strengthen family ties.

Handouts and Resources

All the necessary handouts and resources are found at the end of each chapter in the manual. They are also found on the accompanying CD-ROM, in both color and black-and-white versions. The black-and-white materials may be customized to suit your particular needs.

Facilitating the Sessions

Team Approach

Team members are expected to participate in all the activities, versus "watching" the youth participate. Team members are also expected to reach out to get to know the attendees instead of just relating with each other.

Inviting Youth

The most effective invitation is a personal one—inviting a young person to the session directly, either by phone, e-mail, or direct personal contact. The best invitations come from young people who invite their friends and others to join them at the session.

Hospitality

Hospitality needs to be a part of every aspect of the gathering: in the invitations and promotional materials (by using inclusive language and images), in the welcoming of participants to the session, in the inclusivity of the relationships (in other words, the team members for the session do not hang out just with each other but are prepared to meet and remember as many people as they can), and in the follow-up connected to the event.

Community Building

Although all the sessions in this manual are designed to help build community, adult leaders should decide if additional time needs to be spent on warm-up activities (in other words, activities that will help people feel comfortable or get to know other people's names) to help the participants feel comfortable within the group. Community building fosters the development of relationships between the participants and the team. Warm-up activities help the participants get to know one another in a nonthreatening way, small-group discussions give the participants structured topics around which to build conversation, and one-to-one sharing allows participants to feel comfortable with the group.

Prayer

Prayer helps us remember for whom we are evangelizing and through whom conversion comes. Prayer by the team is encouraged before they welcome the participants and at the end of the session, to integrate the challenges of the session.

Presentations

In each session, leaders will be asked to make presentations to the young people. Ensure that these presentations are effective by practicing them ahead of time, personalizing the materials by adding your own stories and examples, familiarizing yourself with the material, and inviting constructive criticism from other leaders.

Facilitation

The skills of large-group facilitation are important. When working with the young people, the leader of the session or activity should have a strong understanding of the entire session and his or her role within it. He or she should be attentive to the time allotted for each activity and the core purpose of the activity.

Preparing Yourself

Read each session or activity before you facilitate it; then use it creatively to meet the needs of the young people in your group. Knowing your audience will help you determine which activities will work best for it. Some of the activities require preparation. Allow yourself adequate time to get ready.

All the sessions include presentations of key concepts and teachings. The session plans offer guidelines for these talks. Preparing for those presentations is vital to the success of each session.

Standard Materials

To save time, consider gathering frequently used materials in bins and storing those bins in a place that is accessible to all staff and volunteer leaders. Here are some recommendations for organizing the bins.

Supply Bin

The following items appear frequently in the materials checklists:
- *The Catholic Youth Bible,* at least one copy for every two participants
- *The Catholic Faith Handbook for Youth,* for your reference as leader
- masking tape
- cellophane tape
- washable and permanent markers (thick-line and thin-line)
- pens or pencils
- self-stick notes
- scissors
- newsprint
- blank paper, scrap paper, and notebook paper
- journals, one for each participant
- index cards
- baskets
- candles and matches
- items to create a prayer space (for example, a colored cloth, a cross, a bowl of water, and a vase for flowers)

Music Bin

Young people often find profound meaning in the music and lyrics of songs, both past and present. Also, the right music can set the appropriate mood for a prayer or an activity. Begin with a small collection of tapes or CDs in a music bin, and add to it over time. You might ask the young people to put some of their favorite music in the bin. The bin might include the following styles of music:
- *Prayerful, reflective instrumental music,* such as the kind that is available in the adult alternative section of music stores. Labels that specialize in this type of music include Windham Hill and Narada.
- *Popular songs with powerful messages.* If you are not well versed in popular music, ask the young people to offer suggestions.
- *The music of contemporary Catholic artists.* Many teens are familiar with the work of Catholic musicians such as Steve Angrisano, Sarah Hart, David W. Kauffman, Michael Mahler, Jesse Manibusan, and Danielle Rose.

Also consider including songbooks and hymnals. Many of the musical selections suggested in Total Youth Ministry are taken from the *Spirit & Song* hymnal, published by Oregon Catholic Press (OCP). If you wish to order copies of this hymnal, please contact OCP directly at *www.ocp.org* or by calling 800-548-8749. Including copies of your parish's chosen hymnal is a suitable option as well. You might also check with your liturgy or music director for recordings of parish hymns.

Some Closing Thoughts

We hope you find this material helpful as you invite young people into a deeper relationship with the marvelous community of faith we know as the Catholic Church. Please be assured of our continual prayers for you and the young people you serve.

Your Comments or Suggestions

Saint Mary's Press wants to know your reactions to the materials in the Total Youth Ministry series. We are open to all kinds of suggestions, including these:
- an alternative way to conduct an activity
- an audiovisual or other media resource that worked well with this material
- a book or an article you found helpful
- an original activity or process
- a prayer experience or service
- a helpful preparation for other leaders
- an observation about the themes or content of this material

If you have a comment or suggestion, please write to us at 702 Terrace Heights, Winona, MN 55987-1318; call us at our toll-free number, 800-533-8095; or e-mail us at *smp@smp.org*. Your ideas will help improve future editions of Total Youth Ministry.

Part A
Introductory Article

1 Community Is Essential to Youth Ministry

Relationships are the starting point for youth ministry. Most young people's involvement in Church life, including youth ministry, is directly related to the sense of welcome they experience as members of the parish community and as participants in youth ministry programming. When relationships among youth and between youth and adults are left to chance, they have as much potential for failure as they have for success. To be a Christian community—the Body of Christ—we must be attentive to the welcome, acceptance, and invitation to participation that each young person receives. *Renewing the Vision* states:

> The content of our message will be heard only when it is lived in our relationships and community life. To teach compassion, generosity, tolerance, peace, forgiveness, acceptance, and love as gospel values and to identify ourselves as Christians requires us to live these values in our interactions with young people and in our community life. (P. 34)

This quotation makes it clear that it is impossible to teach the faith if it is not lived out within our communities. This is especially true for young people who are searching for faith and learning judgment skills. If our parish communities talk about being the Body of Christ but do not act on those beliefs, young people can become disillusioned. However, if our parish communities and youth ministry programs welcome young people with open arms, are attentive to their needs, provide opportunities for intergenerational and peer relationships, and create space for their questions and ideas, then young people experience the love of God and find meaning within their Catholic faith.

> All our efforts at building community must be based on Gospel values and be imbedded in our parish structures. In 2002, the "Effective Youth Ministry Practices in Catholic Parishes" research project uncovered the following information. When asked, "What works in youth

What Do You Think?

Is our parish being attentive to the welcoming, acceptance, and invitation to participation that each young person in our parish should receive?

ministry?" adult leaders, parish staffs, and youth responded with the following ideas:
- Hospitality and relationship building are foundational to effective youth ministry.
- Young people are welcomed and accepted.
- Extending personal invitations, providing a warm welcome, building relationships, and forming groups is intentional and ongoing.
- A web of relationships is created: youth with youth, youth with adults, parish community with youth, youth with their families.

Renewing the Vision speaks of youth-friendly communities as a way to describe a parish that is willing to reach out and minister to every young person through all the ministries of the parish. Such parishes value young people, see youth as a resource, and provide opportunities for intergenerational relationships:

> If parishes are to be worthy of the loyalty and active participation of youth, they will need to become "youth-friendly" communities in which youth have a conspicuous presence in parish life. (P. 13)

What Do You Think?
- Do we give as much attention to the role of the parish as we do to our youth ministry programs?
- What are the things that hold us back from making our parish youth-friendly?

The role of the parish in the life of a young person is of equal importance to the role of the youth ministry program. Something is missing when a young person experiences welcome and acceptance within a youth ministry program, but finds themselves excluded and their needs pushed aside within the larger parish community. The whole parish is responsible for providing ministry to youth, and if only a few people are taking that responsibility to heart, it will be reflected in the parish's relationship with its young people. *Renewing the Vision* reminds us, "The ministry of community is not only *what* we do (activity), but *who* we are (identity), and *how* we interact (relationships)" (p. 34). We must create an atmosphere in which *all* youth feel welcomed, safe, and appreciated. This cannot be true only within a small setting of the faith community, like the youth ministry program, but must also be true in all elements of parish life.

Community life comprises three important elements: atmosphere, attitude, and actions. It is essential to create an atmosphere in which young people know they are safe and accepted. They need to know that their presence is valued, their energy is appreciated, and they are invited and welcomed to contribute their own ideas and skills within the community.

> I think those sorts of settings, right music, right context can really help them to be able to open up and to pray too. Somehow the setting has to be such that they sort of can forget about themselves. (Quote from an adult leader, "Effective Practices")

The attitude of all community members toward its young must be authentic (young people can spot a phony a mile off), positive, and understanding. In addition, what we say and do (or what we don't say or do) communicates volumes to young people. Parish communities and programs that are inviting and supportive and that help young people get to know others and build trusting relationships will be authentic Christian communities.

Building community is not the end goal of our ministry, but our goals cannot be accomplished without community. All people of faith come to know God through other people and are challenged to grow in faith through involvement in community. Within Catholic youth ministry, we have named our primary goals: creating disciples, encouraging involvement in the work and mission of the Church, and developing faithful individuals who live with a depth of spirituality and a healthy sense of self. These goals will only be achieved in a network of relationships, in other words, within a community. Young people in particular need to *experience* faith: engage in service activities, pray in community, hear about faith journeys in story and conversation, and see how friends and mentors express their faith in everyday life. By building community among young people, they will be able to walk through adolescence—a time of dramatic change—with friends and guides.

Young people will be able to learn from their peers, find refuge in common struggles, and provide direction and insight to others who are at a different place on their faith journey. When we are intentional about building community intergenerationally, we give young people the opportunity to learn about discipleship through the lived experience of faithful adults, find consolation and support from others outside their families, and provide guides and mentors as they move from childhood into adulthood. Relationships with adults help young people move through this transition with success.

> A recent report, *Grading Grown-Ups 2002: How Do American Kids and Adults Relate?* (a national study by Search Institute with support from Thrivent Financial for Lutherans), highlights this issue:
>
> > There is clear evidence that young people benefit from multiple, sustained relationships with adults outside their immediate family. For example, Search Institute research has found that the more adults a young person reports that he or she can turn to, the better off that young person is. Yet just 22 percent of the youth surveyed reported having strong relationships with five or more adults other than their parents. (P. 5)

What Do You Think?
- If we gave a report card to our parish's attitude toward young people, what would be our grade?
- What are the actions we should add or subtract that can help young people feel more included and welcomed within our parish?
- Is our parish atmosphere youth-friendly?

What Do You Think?
- What joys of community have we witnessed within our youth community?

The importance of intergenerational ministry should not be overlooked. Parishes can achieve this goal by transforming various youth-only programs and strategies into intergenerational programs and strategies. Parishes can also encourage and provide leadership opportunities for youth within all the parish's ministries—social, liturgical, service, and so forth. In addition, new programs and strategies may be created to build community among all the generations of the parish community.

This vision of our ministry points to the importance of all the components of comprehensive youth ministry, but does not serve as a reason to ignore the need for community building. Developing community life is a noble purpose for youth ministry leaders to embrace. Building community should not be an afterthought or viewed as a frivolous activity. To believe this is to shortchange the next generation from the life-giving message of the Gospel that was first told in community and is only made real today in relationships.

> Read Mark 9:36–37, and then offer the following prayer:
>
> God,
> help me to reach outside of myself,
> to be extra conscious of the young who ache
> to feel connected to you
> and to your people.
> Help me to welcome as you welcome,
> not just with "hello"
> but rather
> with a true and authentic sense of welcome
> that honors, reveres,
> and recognizes that you are with us,
> in all things, in all people.
> Help me to see you in them.
> Amen.
>
> (David Haas, *Finding the Calm*, p. 39)

Part B
Community Life Sessions

2 Let's Get Started

Overview

This session can be used at the beginning of a program year, at the start of a retreat, in preparation for a mission trip, or at any other time and place where helping people know and trust one another is important. It is designed for participants who do not know one another, although it can be easily adapted for use with groups who are more familiar. This session follows the outline for community building that is available in chapter 12 of this manual.

Outcomes

- The participants will have the opportunity to get to know one another.
- The participants will be encouraged to open themselves up to others by sharing personal information.
- The participants will investigate what it means to be a Christian community.

Background Reading

- Scriptural connections: Acts 2:43–47 (life among the believers), 1 Cor. 12:12–30 (one body with many members), Phil. 1:3–11 (Paul's prayer for the Philippians)
- *Catholic Youth Bible* article connections: "Christian Community" (Acts 2:43–47), "Here Comes Everybody" (Acts 10:34–36), "Encouragement" (1 Thess. 3:6–13)

AT A GLANCE

Study It

Core Session:
Let's Get Started
(65 minutes)
- Welcome
  (5 minutes)
- Knots
  (10 minutes)
- Group Juggling
  (10 minutes)
- Nametag Interviews
  (25 minutes)
- Michelangelo
  (15 minutes)

Session Extensions
- Line-Up
  (10 minutes)
- Freeze
  (20 to 30 minutes)

Pray It

- Sculpting Our Prayer to God
  (10 minutes)

Core Session: Let's Get Started (65 minutes)

Preparation
- Gather the following items:
  - ❑ a deck of playing cards (if your group size is more than fifty-two, you will need an additional deck of cards)
  - ❑ nametags, one for each participant
  - ❑ tennis balls, bean bags, plastic toys, or other objects that can be thrown and caught easily; three objects for each small group of eight
  - ❑ colored paper, one sheet for each participant
  - ❑ thin-line markers, one for each participant
  - ❑ newsprint and markers, or a chalkboard and chalk
  - ❑ masking tape
  - ❑ a CD player and a CD of instrumental music
  - ❑ a whistle (optional)
- You will need one small-group leader for every eight participants. The leaders should be familiar with the activities and understand their role as welcomers, encouragers, and small-group leaders. Small-group leaders can be adults or youth.
- Divide the deck of cards into suits. Each person will be asked to find a partner with the same number or face card and the same color. For instance, the person with the two of hearts will need to find the person with the two of diamonds. You will need to have the same number of cards as you have people present. For example, for twenty people, you will need ten pairs of cards.
- You will need a large, open space for some activities, and tables and chairs for writing work.

Welcome (5 minutes)

Greet the participants as they arrive for the session. Invite them to make their own nametag, and to wear it on their chest where everyone can see it. Once everyone has arrived, gather the participants and say something similar to the following comments:
- Welcome! We are happy you are here. It is always a little awkward to be in a group where you do not know people well, so we are going to work together to help you to get to know one another better. We have lots of

fun activities planned to help you find out a little more about the others in this group, but in doing so, you will be sharing a little about yourself too. We look forward to getting to know you better.

Knots (10 minutes)

1. Ask all the participants to gather in groups of eight. Have one leader join each group. The leader's job is to clarify directions and affirm the group's work.

2. Provide the following directions:
- Raise your right hand. Now grab the right hand of someone who is across the circle from you.
- Raise your left hand. Grab the left hand of someone who is across the circle—but not the person whose right hand you are holding.
- As a group, and without letting go of the hands that you are holding, untangle yourself from the knot.
- You may begin.

3. Some groups accomplish this very quickly, while others take longer. If a group finishes quickly, ask them to change places in the circle, and do the activity again.

Group Juggling (10 minutes)

1. Keep the participants in their knot groups. Give each group one object (a ball, a bean bag, or a plastic toy). Going around the circle, ask each group member to say his or her name, so that each small-group member knows the names of the others in their group.

2. Provide the following directions:
- Whoever has the object will be the lead person for this activity. Your job is to throw the object to someone, calling out her or his name.
- The person who catches the object will then throw it to someone else, calling out that person's name.
- This continues until the object has been thrown to everyone.
- When the last person has the object, call out the name of the lead person, and toss her or him the ball. You are now back at the beginning.
- As a group, follow this same pattern so that you will always be receiving the object from the same person and throwing it to the same person.
- If anyone drops the object, or passes it to the wrong person, begin again with the lead person.

Clarify any questions, and begin the activity.

3. After each group has been around the circle at least once, give the lead person an additional object so that he or she has two objects going at the same time. After a minute or two more, give the lead person a third object to pass around their group. This can be done without stopping the action, by simply going to each group individually, giving the lead person the second or third object, and telling him or her to begin using it.

4. After about four minutes, call time and collect the objects.

Nametag Interviews (25 minutes)

1. You will need to use tables and chairs for this activity. Place the colored paper and thin-line markers on the tables. Divide the participants into random pairs by giving each one a playing card. Ask each person to find a partner who has the same number and same color of card. For example, the ten of hearts is paired with the ten of diamonds.

2. Ask each pair to introduce themselves to each other and sit together at one of the tables. Each participant will need a piece of paper and a marker.

3. Tell the participants that they are going to make a large nametag for their partner, following the directions they will be given. Invite a team leader to assist you by demonstrating how to make the nametags on a large sheet of newsprint, hung in the landscape orientation, as you provide the following instructions:

- Your partner is someone we would like you to get to know better. Your job is to interview your partner and create a nametag for him or her.
- Ask your partner what name he or she most likes to be called. It might be their given name or a nickname. Write the name in large print in the middle of the paper.
- In the bottom right-hand corner of the paper, write the name of a fictional character you think your partner is most like.
- In the top left-hand corner, write the name of your partner's favorite band, music CD, or song. You can include the name of the recording artist as well.
- In the top right-hand corner, write the name of the city where your partner was born, the number of houses he or she has lived in, and the name of the community where he or she now lives.
- In the bottom left-hand corner, write a number from 1 to 5 (5 is high) that describes how strong your partner's faith is right now, and one word he or she would use to describe his or her relationship with God.
- In the space at the bottom of the page, write the names of his or her pets (if any) and the people with whom he or she lives.

- In the space at the top of the page, write words that describe your partner—either roles your partner has (student, football player) or adjectives to describe him or her (funny, interesting).

4. When everyone is finished with the nametags, give each person a piece of masking tape, and ask them to tape the nametag to their shirt.

5. Ask everyone to stand and gather in an open area. Play some instrumental music during this time to encourage silence. Give the following instructions:
- You will need to be *silent* for this next activity. Your job is to mingle throughout the room, looking at the nametags that were created for each individual.
- Look at the nametags carefully, because you will be asked to find someone to talk to whose nametag interests you. Try to look at as many nametags as possible.
- I will let you know when your time is up.

Allow 3 to 5 minutes for the group to mingle. At the end of the time, ask the participants to find someone in the group whom they did not know before and whom they would now like to meet, perhaps because of something intriguing they saw on the nametag. When everyone has found a partner, invite the pairs to sit down (either on the floor or in chairs), introduce themselves, and talk about their nametags and the information that interested them. Allow about 3 minutes for this discussion.

6. Invite the participants, one at a time, to share the interesting information they saw on other people's nametags or that they heard in the discussion with their partner. Someone might say: "I saw lots of people who like the same band that I do. I was surprised by that." You may want to ask for the name of the band and see how many other people like that band as well.

7. Conclude the activity with the following comments:
- Thank you for taking the risk of sharing with so many different people. Your willingness to share with the others in the room helps us to get to know one another and become comfortable within our group.
- We are going to collect your nametags so these works of art that were created for you do not get ruined in our next activity.

Tell the participants what you will do with the nametags: decorate the walls of the room, use them as nameplates on doors of retreat or religious education rooms, or hand them back to the individuals at the end of the session. Collect the nametags.

TryThis

If this session is used at the start of a retreat or other longer event, the nametags that are created can be used as nameplates for bedroom doors. If the session is used at the start of an ongoing ministry effort, the nametags can decorate the meeting space for the rest of the program year.

Michelangelo (15 minutes)

Preparation
- This activity sets the stage for a component of the closing prayer. Be familiar with the directions for the prayer prior to the start of this activity, so that one leader can keep track of which groups they want to represent the different sculptures during the prayer. Write down the names of the individuals selected and the name of their sculpture.
- This activity will involve young people touching each other. If you notice that a participant is uncomfortable, ask that participant to help the leader, who is the observer.

1. Tell the participants that they will be working with the same partner they had in the previous activity. Ask everyone to stand with her or his partner. Then give the following instructions:
- Who has the higher house number?
- If you have the higher house number, you are now Michelangelo, the first sculptor for your group.
- If you are the person with the lower house number, you have become a lump of clay. As a lump of clay, you are not able to speak.
- Michelangelo's job is to form the lump of clay into a sculpture that expresses an emotion. Lumps of clay are very cooperative, and move easily when directed.
- Michelangelos, you have only 15 seconds to sculpt your lumps of clay. When time is called, your clay must freeze in position. Then you will sit down so everyone can admire your sculpture. (At the end of each round, the whole group will be asked to select its favorite sculpture.)
- These sculptures will be used in our closing prayer. If you are selected as a favorite sculpture, please try to remember your pose.
- Because this is a Catholic activity, let's make sure the sculptures are appropriate—and that we are careful about how we touch other people.
- Do you have any questions?

2. Begin the first round by saying the following:
- Michelangelos: Form lumps of clay into sculptures depicting *laughter*. You have 15 seconds.

Conduct a 5-second countdown and then call time (perhaps by blowing a whistle). Ask the clay forms to freeze and the Michelangelos to sit down. Invite the group to comment on the sculptures, and then take a quick vote to see which sculpture best depicts *laughter*.

3. For the next round, have the pairs switch roles so that the lumps of clay become Michelangelos, and the Michelangelos become the clay. Then say the following:

- Michelangelos: Mold your clay into a sculpture depicting *fear*. You have 15 seconds.

Conduct a 5-second countdown and then call time. Ask the clay forms to freeze and the Michelangelos to sit down. Invite the group to comment on the sculptures, and then take a quick vote to see which sculpture best depicts *fear*.

4. Ask each pair to join with another pair, to form groups of four. Ask members of these new groups to introduce themselves and to find out which two people have birthdays closest to today's date. These two will be Michelangelos. Explain that there will now be two lumps of clay and two Michelangelos. Then say:

- Michelangelos: Work together to form your lumps of clay into a sculpture depicting *trust*. You have 20 seconds.

Conduct a 5-second countdown and then call time. Ask the clay forms to freeze and the Michelangelos to sit down. Invite the group to comment on the sculptures, and then take a quick vote to see which sculpture best depicts *trust*.

5. Ask the Michelangelos and the lumps of clay to switch roles. Then say:

- Michelangelos: Mold your clay into a sculpture depicting *companionship*. You have 20 seconds.

Conduct a 5-second countdown and then call time. Ask the clay forms to freeze and the Michelangelos to sit down. Invite the group to comment on the sculptures, and then take a quick vote to see which sculpture best depicts *companionship*.

6. Ask each group of four to join another group, to form groups of eight. Members of the newly formed groups should introduce themselves. Explain that everyone will now be both Michelangelo and a lump of clay at the same time. That means they will have to work together to form a sculpture using all eight people. Each group selects one person to act as the group spokesperson, who will explain their sculpture. Before the sculpting begins, have all the spokespersons raise their hand so you can be sure that all the groups have one. Then say:

- Form a sculpture depicting *Christian community*. You have 30 seconds.

Announce when 15 seconds are left, conduct a 5-second countdown, and then call time. Ask all the participants to freeze.

7. Going group by group, ask the spokesperson to explain his or her group's sculpture. When a group has explained its sculpture, its members can sit and watch as the other groups' sculptures are explained. End by congratulating the participants on their good work and making the following comments:

- Getting to know one another, laughing together, and beginning to trust one another are important parts of creating Christian community. Christian community means that we accept, support, and are connected to one another through our common faith in Jesus Christ.
- It is hoped that these activities have helped us get to know one another a little better, and made all of us feel more comfortable with one another.

Session Extensions

Line-Up (10 minutes)

1. Gather the participants into a common open area. Point out an "imaginary line" that divides the room. Explain that you will be giving them two choices, and that they have to choose one side of the line or the other. They are not allowed to stand on the line; they have to make a choice.

2. Stand on the imaginary line and point to one side of the room while announcing one choice, and then point to the other side of the room and announce the other choice. Once you have announced both choices, the participants are free to move to either side of the room. The choices are as follows:
- Are you more of a morning person (left side) or an evening person (right side)?
- Are you someone who will eat almost anything or are you a picky eater?
- Are you more like Mickey Mouse or Goofy?
- Would you prefer a vacation at the beach or in the mountains?
- Are you more like McDonald's or Taco Bell?
- Are you more like baseball or downhill skiing?
- Would you rather have a salad or a steak?
- Would you describe yourself as religious or as spiritual?
- Would you rather read a book or watch a movie?
- Are you more of a listener or a talker?
- Are you more like a banana split or a Blizzard?
- Are you more of a leader or a follower?
- Would you prefer a sunny day or a star-filled night?
- Are you more like James Bond or Austin Powers?

3. As you announce each choice, stop and ask if anyone would like to tell the others why they have made their particular choice. If the participants seem anxious to tell about their choices, stop each time. If it seems to quiet the group or make them nervous, do not ask for verbal feedback. When the activity is done, ask the group what they learned about the others or about themselves.

4. Conclude this activity with the following comments:
- There is a lot we do not know about one another, and this activity gives us some insight into what other people would choose or what they think about themselves.
- There are lots of ways to get to know one another. Perhaps this activity will give you a starting point for talking to someone new in this room.

Freeze (20 to 30 minutes)

Preparation
- Use a large, open space where the participants can sit or stand in a circle.

1. Recruit two volunteers from the participants. Ask them to come forward into the center of the circle. Then explain the activity to the participants in this way:
- This game is called Freeze. We will start with [names of volunteers], and I will give both of them an action they have to act out. For instance, I might say "dancing," and they would have to dance.
- I will call "freeze" after a short time. When I call freeze, both [names of volunteers] must freeze.
- I will then ask for a new volunteer to take the place of either [name of volunteer] or [name of volunteer]. The new volunteer must physically take the place of the person they are replacing, and then engage the other person in a new activity (different from dancing). They can communicate the new activity through words or actions, and the other person should join them in acting out the activity. Once again, after a short time, I will call freeze.
- Each time freeze is called, I will look for a new volunteer to take the place of one of the participants who is in the circle. It is up to the new volunteer to determine what the new activity will be, so don't volunteer unless you have a creative idea and are ready to get started as soon as you take the place of one of the two people in the circle.
- Once an activity (dancing, for instance) has been done in the circle, it cannot be done again, unless we start over.
- Do you have any questions?

Most groups have some "actors" in the crowd, who will easily jump into this activity. As time goes on, however, those who are less inclined to participate are often willing to volunteer. Pay attention to who is volunteering, and invite those who have not previously volunteered. People can volunteer more than one time, but do not neglect to invite those who don't volunteer to join the activity.

2. Tell the two volunteers to begin with "figure skating."

Sculpting Our Prayer to God (10 minutes)

Preparation
- Gather the following items:
  - ❑ a *Catholic Youth Bible* or other Bible, marked at Isa. 64:8
- Gather the individuals whose sculptures were selected from the Michelangelo activity. Work with the "clays" for a few minutes before the prayer to help them remember what their pose was and to explain how they will be participating in the prayer.
- Ask a participant to proclaim the reading.

    1. Gather the participants in a semicircle, creating a "stage" area for the sculptures. Those participating in the sculptures should be close to the front, but still a part of the whole group. Get the group's attention, and let them know that prayer will be a little different today. Begin with the following information:

- We can pray to God in many different ways. Today we will use our Michelangelo sculptures to help us pray.
- You might find that you want to smile or laugh during the prayer, and that is fine, as long as it helps us celebrate our relationship with God. Please don't get too silly, however, and distract others from praying together.
- We will begin with the sign of the cross, which is used throughout the world by Catholics. It is a sign of our common faith in God. After each prayer, please repeat the expression of gratitude.

    2. Invite the reader to come forward and proclaim the Scripture passage. Allow a few moments for quiet reflection.

    3. Invite the first sculpture to come up front and take his or her pose as *laughter*. Then say:

- Lord, there has been much laughter during our time together. Thank you for giving us these moments of joy when we are free to be ourselves, to really enjoy one another's company, and to laugh and smile. And so we pray, "Thank you, Lord, for the gift of laughter." (Gesture for the participants to repeat the phrase you have just spoken.)

4. Invite the second sculpture to come up front and take her or his pose as *fear.* Say to the group:

- Lord, coming here we had some fear about what would happen. We weren't sure if we would be accepted or liked, or if we would enjoy our time with these new people. Thank you for helping us walk through the fear to arrive at this new place of comfort we have with one another. And so we pray, "Thank you, Lord, for helping us overcome our fear." (Gesture for the participants to repeat the phrase you have just spoken.)

5. Invite the third sculpture to come up front and take his or her pose as *trust.* Say to the group:

- Lord, we know that community isn't really possible without trust. We know that you live in each of us and that our relationship with you gives us a common bond. We offer thanks for helping us trust one another and for giving us the opportunity to know one another better. And so we pray, "Help us, Lord, to continue to trust one another." (Gesture for the participants to repeat the phrase you have just spoken.)

6. Invite the fourth sculpture to come up front and take their pose as *companionship.* Say to the group:

- Lord, we know we need friends on our journey of life and faith. We will not grow as people of faith without others to encourage and challenge us. We offer to you the hope that we have found some people within this group who will be companions on our journey of life and faith. And so we pray, "Help us, Lord, to be open to the new people you send into our lives." (Gesture for the participants to repeat the phrase you have just spoken.)

7. Invite the last sculpture to come up front and take their pose as *Christian community.* Say to the group:

- Lord, we have spent only a short time together, but we know you call us to community in every part of our lives. Help us to be as much a community with these people in the coming weeks as we have been today. May we carry this experience of community into our schools and neighborhoods. And so we pray, "Lord, help us to be a Christian community." (Gesture for the participants to repeat the phrase you have just spoken.)

8. Conclude this prayer with "Amen," and invite the participants to offer each other a sign of peace.

3 Who Am I?

AT A GLANCE

Study It

Core Session: "I Am . . ."
(55 minutes)
- True Color Cards
  (15 minutes)
- Color Groups
  (30 minutes)
- Jesus Was Human
  (10 minutes)

Session Extensions
- We Are Many Parts
  (20 minutes)
- Signs and Symbols
  (30 minutes)

Pray It
- Child of God
  (10 minutes)

Live It
- Looking at friends
- Using your gifts

Overview

This session provides young people with an opportunity to learn more about themselves—what makes them unique and what makes them like others. The participants are invited to recognize and value the gifts they have, to know that these gifts are from God, and to realize that the use of their gifts contributes positively to the communities in which they are involved, including their school, their local community, their parish, and the Church as a whole.

Outcomes

- The participants will identify personal gifts, talents, traits, and characteristics.
- The participants will understand how each individual's gifts are essential and integral to any community, organization, or group.
- The participants will explore Jesus' gifts, talents, traits, and characteristics.

Background Reading

- Scriptural connections: Matt. 5:1–12 (the Sermon on the Mount), Matt. 25:14–30 (the parable of the talents)
- *Catholic Youth Bible* article connections: "God's Mysterious Name" (Exod. 3:13–15), "Black and Beautiful" (Song of Sol. 1:5), "It's What's Inside That Counts" (2 Cor. 5:1–5)

Core Session: "I Am . . ." (55 minutes)

Preparation
- Gather the following items:
  ❏ newsprint
  ❏ colored markers, about twelve
- You will need to copy or print out resource 1, "True Color Cards," on colored paper (use a different-colored paper for each one). Cut the pages along the dotted lines, and paper clip the color cards together so that each participant will receive a packet containing one of each of the four cards.

True Color Cards (15 minutes)

1. Begin by making the following comments:
- There are four basic personality groups into which people can be divided.
- We shall call these groups orange, gold, blue, and green.
- Each person has parts of all four colors within them, but each person also has one primary color, one that best describes that person.
- This session is an opportunity for each of us to think about our personality and our "true color."

2. Distribute to each of the participants a packet of four cards. Invite them to read over the cards and place them in order from 1 to 4.
- 1 = the color card that best describes them
- 4 = the color card that least describes them

3. Remind the participants, if necessary, that each person has some of all four colors in them; they are only trying to figure out which color is primary for them. Invite the participants to focus on the descriptive words on each card to help them make their decision.

As the participants are ordering their cards, they may find it easier to identify their primary color by talking to others who know them rather than to decide on their own.

Color Groups (30 minutes)

1. When all the participants have decided on their primary color, divide them into the four color groups: orange, gold, blue, and green. If any group is larger than ten people, subdivide those groups. If a color group has only one participant, invite that person to go to the color group that was her or his second choice.

2. Give each small group a sheet of newsprint and markers, and ask them to create a poster representing or describing their color's personality. They can draw pictures, compile a word list, make an outline, and so on. They may use their cards for guidance. Give each group about 10 minutes to work on their poster.

3. Gather all the participants into a large group, then make the following comments:
- Each small group will have an opportunity to present their poster to the large group.
- Notice the differences between the way the posters were created and the style in which they are presented.
- Pay attention to the people who make up each color group. You will have the opportunity to discover and comment on similarities and differences among the color groups during the discussion time.

4. Invite each group to present its color to the other participants. If there is more than one group for a color, have all groups from the same element make their presentation consecutively.

5. After the presentations are finished, have the participants discuss the following questions:
- What was unique about the orange group?
- What was unique about the gold group?
- What was unique about the green group?
- What was unique about the blue group?
- Why is it important to have all four true colors represented in our communities?
- What would happen to our world if it were made up of only one or two of these groups of people?

6. Make the following comments as a way to move the group into the next activity:
- Each color has something important to offer. Each person needs all four colors, and each community or organization needs all four colors.
- Think of what would happen if we had only gold in the world—or only orange or blue or green. Think of your sports teams, your school, your family, your friends, and your parish. It would be difficult to accomplish anything if there were only one kind of person!
- Sometimes it is easier to recognize other people's strengths and minimize our own. But we are each called to use our own gifts in this life. Our strengths are a gift from God, and other people in our lives can complement our weaknesses.

- Some people, as they grow older, find that their strengths have broadened—they find a little of each of the colors in their personality. However, some people become more focused on one of the colors, finding comfort in their niche. As you grow you will discover your own path in life.

Jesus Was Human (10 minutes)

1. Invite the participants to return to their color groups. Ask them to share their responses to the following questions:
- How is Jesus like your small group's color?
- In which story from the Scriptures does Jesus appear to be living out your group's color?

Depending on the biblical literacy of the participants, each group might need some assistance with the second question from a facilitator. The facilitator should be familiar with Gospel stories about Jesus, and should be ready to help participants think of stories they know about Jesus and make connections from them to some of the strengths of each color. Give the groups about 5 minutes to discuss the two questions.

2. Gather the participants into a large group. Ask each color group to share with the large group how Jesus lived out their color, by giving examples from Jesus' life and talking about the Bible story they chose.

3. Make the following comments:
- Jesus was human, and so, just like us, he had a part of each of the colors in him. We saw this in the examples that you gave about him and in the stories that were captured in the Bible about how he lived.
- Jesus was also God, and so, unlike us, he was able to live from each of the colors—moving seamlessly between them. Jesus knew how to relate to many different people, using the strengths he possessed in all the color areas.
- Because Jesus lived and acted from each of the colors, he knows our strengths and knows what is difficult for us. Jesus can be both a model for us of how to live and a support to us as we learn and discover more about ourselves.

Session Extensions

We Are Many Parts (20 minutes)

Preparation
- Gather the following items:
  - ❏ paper and pencils, one of each for each small group
  - ❏ a small prize for the winning group (optional)
  - ❏ a *Catholic Youth Bible* or other Bible, marked at 1 Cor. 12:12–20

1. Gather the participants into their color groups (or use random groups, if desired). Give each group a piece of paper and a pencil. Tell the participants:
- This activity is a race between the groups.
- The first group to correctly complete the activity is the winner (and will get a prize).
- The object of the activity is to list ten body parts that have only three letters. Crude or slang terms do not count.

Give the groups up to 5 minutes to complete their task. If no group has all ten body parts by the end of the 5 minutes, give winner status to the group that has the most. The answers: eye, ear, lip, jaw, gum, arm, leg, hip, toe, and rib.

2. Lead a discussion on the following questions:
- What do all ten body parts have in common?
- How do these parts function together?
- How are the parts of the body similar to the Church?
- If one part is missing, how does that affect the body? the Church?
- What are some of the different "parts" that make up the Church? Which part is your favorite?

3. If not brought out in the discussion, make the following comments:
- The Church is made up of the many different gifts and talents that make up the people of God. The Church is less if it does not have each of us as an active participant, because the unique ideas, interests, and questions we share make the Church whole.
- Just like the body, if the Church is missing a part, it will have to compensate for it in different ways. (You may want to be honest here about the parts of the Church that are weak in your parish—especially if the young people have already named them—or you may choose to talk about the things that are strong in the parish.)
- God has called us together to be "the Body of Christ," which means that it is our responsibility, right here and right now, to be Jesus in the world. We are Jesus' hands, feet, heart, and head.

4. Close with the Scripture reading.

(This activity is adapted from *Jumpstarters*, p. 10.)

Signs and Symbols (30 minutes)

Preparation
- Gather the following items:
  - ❏ newsprint and tape
  - ❏ colored markers, about five for each small group

1. Gather the participants into their color groups. Give each group a sheet of newsprint and markers. Make the following comments:
- Today we looked at four primary personality types, and used colors to help us talk about our strengths and weaknesses.
- As a Church, we often use ordinary things to help us understand the mysteries of God. For instance, we use the four primary elements—water, earth, fire, and wind—as a part of our sacraments and our Church life.

2. Assign each of the color groups one of the primary elements (water, earth, fire, or wind). Invite each group to depict visually how their element appears in nature. For example, water may be represented as rain, a lake, a river, a flood, or a creek. Earth may be represented as dirt, mountains, plants, or trees. Fire may be represented as a campfire, a forest fire, a fireplace, or a candle. Wind may be represented as clouds, blowing leaves in the air, a tornado, or swirls of snow. Give the small groups 5 minutes to prepare their posters.

3. Have each small group share its poster with the large group, and tape it up on the wall. You will want all the posters on one wall or part of one wall. The second set of posters (in the next part of the activity) should be placed close to these, but in a separate space.

4. Regather in color element groups. Give each small group another sheet of newsprint. Ask them to list or draw on their newsprint the ways their element is used within our faith. Some examples may include: Water symbolizes Baptism, cleansing of sins, purity, and sprinkling rites. Earth symbolizes ashes, bread, wine, and oil. Fire symbolizes candles in church, baptismal and Confirmation candles, the Easter candle, the new fire at the Easter Vigil, light, and goodness. Wind symbolizes the Holy Spirit, Pentecost, music, the Scriptures and teachings flowing to our ears, the sacrament of Confirmation, and incense.

5. Invite each group to share their poster with the large group, and post it on the wall.

6. Gather the young people so they can view both sets of posters, and ask them to respond to the following questions:
- Why does our Church use the same elements that appear in nature? For example, we use water to bathe or shower, and we feel clean and refreshed. So, too, does the water of Baptism cleanse and refresh us. The Church uses these elements to connect our spiritual and lived experiences.
- Like our personal traits that we talked about earlier, why is it so important to have all these elements in nature? in the Church?

7. Conclude the activity with the following comments:
- Our Church's signs and symbols come from the lived experience of the people of God throughout the centuries. We experience God in a beautiful sunset, a mountain, a friend's embrace, and the miracle of a baby.
- Many of the symbols we use in Church—oil, candles, water—do not hold the same significance for us as they did for earlier generations—because our light comes from lightbulbs, our water flows throughout our house, and we no longer need oil in the same way. Each of us has been in the dark at one time or another—outdoors or when the power goes off in our home, for example. It is easy to understand how significant light is when you turn on your flashlight or light a candle.
- In the coming weeks, as you interact with the signs and symbols of our Church, try to be open to the ways in which they, like a beautiful sunset, can help us experience God in a more concrete, tangible way.

Spirit & Song connections

- "We Gotta Love," by Tom Booth, Israel Houghton, and Matt Maher
- "Thy Word Is a Lamp," by Michael W. Smith
- "This Little Light of Mine," an African spiritual

Child of God (10 minutes)

Preparation
- Gather the following items:
  - ❏ a *Catholic Youth Bible* or other Bible, marked at Exod. 3:1–7,10–14
  - ❏ one copy of resource 2, "Our Deepest Fear"
  - ❏ copies of handout 1, "Color Prayer," one for each participant
  - ❏ a CD player and a music CD
  - ❏ a prayer table with the following symbols:
    - ☐ a tabletop water fountain or a glass bowl of water (to represent water)
    - ☐ a bowl of dirt (to represent the earth)
    - ☐ a candle (to represent fire)
    - ☐ a pinwheel or wind chimes (to represent wind)
- Invite a participant to proclaim the Scripture passage Exod. 3:1–7,10–14
- Ask a participant to proclaim the reflection from resource 2, "Our Deepest Fear."
- Invite one person from each of the four color groups to read the petition for their group from handout 1, "Color Prayer."
- Choose an opening song, preferably "Who Am I," by Point of Grace (on John Tesh's *One World* CD, Gts Records, 1999), or another song with a self-identity theme.

1. Gather the participants around the prayer table. Begin by inviting the participants to either listen to or join in singing the opening song you have chosen.

2. Say something similar to the following:
- Today we have spent time discovering more about ourselves. We have acknowledged our strengths and our weaknesses. We gather together today realizing that discovering "Who Am I?" will be a lifelong journey, but one that we do in the company of Jesus, our model for living. Let us listen to the Scripture reading.

3. Invite the reader to come forward to proclaim the Scripture reading. Allow a few moments of silence to follow.

4. Invite those you have asked to be readers to continue with the prayer petitions as noted on handout 1, "Color Prayer."

Options and Actions

- **Looking at friends.** Suggest that the participants take the time to observe the different *colors* in their friends, clubs, teams, and organizations. They will begin to notice how each person brings different gifts and talents to the group. Suggest that they take the time to tell their friends or group members about the gifts they see in them, and to discuss ways to utilize these gifts as they work or play together.
- **Using your gifts.** Invite the young people to connect their gifts and talents to the parish community. Use this session as a way to invite people into further participation.

Familyconnections

- Invite the participants to take the color cards home. Each member of the family can choose their true color. Encourage families to talk about the following questions: How do these colors work together to create family harmony? When is it difficult for these colors to work together?
- Suggest that the participants write a note to a family member that includes the values she or he appreciates in that person.
- Invite participants to play the "We Are Many Parts" game (naming the ten body parts that are only three letters long) with their families. The family members can work as individuals or as teams. Encourage the families to talk about the following questions: How are all the parts of the body necessary? What are the different roles that each person plays within the family?

True Color Cards

I Am . . . BLUE! *Words that describe me:* Enthusiastic, sympathetic, personal: I look for meaning and significance in life. Warm, communicative, compassionate: I need to contribute, to encourage, and to care. Idealistic, spiritual, sincere: I value integrity and unity in relationships. Peaceful, flexible, imaginative: I am a natural romantic, a poet, a nurturer.

As a child: I was extremely imaginative, and found it difficult to fit into the structure of school life. I reacted with great sensitivity to discordance or rejection, and sought recognition.

At school and at work: I have a strong desire to influence others so they may lead more significant lives. I often work in the arts, communications, education, and the helping professions. I am adept at motivating and interacting with others.

In relationships: I seek harmonious relationships. I am a true romantic, and believe in perfect love that lasts forever. I bring drama, warmth, and empathy to all relationships. I enjoy the symbols of romance, such as flowers, candlelight, and music, and cherish small gestures of love.

(This resource is taken from Don Lowry's *True Colors* [Laguna Beach, CA: Communication Companies, International]. All rights reserved. Used with permission.)

I Am . . . BLUE! *Words that describe me:* Enthusiastic, sympathetic, personal: I look for meaning and significance in life. Warm, communicative, compassionate: I need to contribute, to encourage, and to care. Idealistic, spiritual, sincere: I value integrity and unity in relationships. Peaceful, flexible, imaginative: I am a natural romantic, a poet, a nurturer.

As a child: I was extremely imaginative, and found it difficult to fit into the structure of school life. I reacted with great sensitivity to discordance or rejection, and sought recognition.

At school and at work: I have a strong desire to influence others so they may lead more significant lives. I often work in the arts, communications, education, and the helping professions. I am adept at motivating and interacting with others.

In relationships: I seek harmonious relationships. I am a true romantic, and believe in perfect love that lasts forever. I bring drama, warmth, and empathy to all relationships. I enjoy the symbols of romance, such as flowers, candlelight, and music, and cherish small gestures of love.

(This resource is taken from Don Lowry's *True Colors* [Laguna Beach, CA: Communication Companies, International]. All rights reserved. Used with permission.)

I Am . . . GOLD!

Words that describe me: Loyal, dependable, prepared: I have a strong sense of what is right and wrong in life. Thorough, sensible, punctual: I need to be useful and to belong. Faithful, stable, organized: I value home, family, and tradition. Caring, concerned, concrete: I am a natural preserver, a parent, a helper.

As a child: I wanted to follow the rules and regulations of the school. I understood and respected authority, and was comfortable with academic routine. I was the easiest of all types of children to adapt to the educational system.

At school and at work: I provide stability and can maintain organization. My ability to handle details and work hard makes me the backbone of many organizations. I believe that work comes before play, even if I must work overtime to complete the job.

In relationships: I am serious, and tend to have traditional, conservative views of both love and marriage. I want a mate who can work along with me to build a secure, predictable life together. I demonstrate love and affection through the practical things I do for my loved ones.

(This resource is taken from Don Lowry's *True Colors* [Laguna Beach, CA: Communication Companies, International]. All rights reserved. Used with permission.)

I Am . . . ORANGE!

Words that describe me: Witty, charming, spontaneous: I think of life as a game, here and now. Impulsive, generous, impactful: I need fun, variety, stimulation, and excitement. Optimistic, eager, bold: I value skill, resourcefulness, and courage. Physical, immediate, fraternal: I am a natural trouble-shooter, a performer, a competitor.

As a child: I had the most difficult time fitting into an academic routine. I learn by doing and experiencing, rather than by listening and reading. I need physical involvement in the learning process, and am motivated by my naturally competitive nature and sense of fun.

At school and at work: I am bored and restless with jobs that are routine and structured. I am satisfied in careers that allow more independence and freedom while utilizing my physical coordination and my love of tools. I am a natural performer.

In relationships: I seek a relationship with shared activities and interests. With my mate, I like to explore new ways to energize the relationship. I enjoy giving extravagant gifts that bring obvious pleasure to my loved ones.

(This resource is taken from Don Lowry's *True Colors* [Laguna Beach, CA: Communication Companies, International]. All rights reserved. Used with permission.)

I Am . . . GREEN!

Words that describe me: Analytical, global, conceptual: I live life by my own standards. Cool, calm, collected: I need explanations and answers. Inventive, logical, perfectionist: I value intelligence, insight, fairness, and justice. Abstract, hypothetical, investigative: I am a natural nonconformist, a visionary, and a problem solver.

As a child: I appeared to be older than my years, and focused on my greatest interest: achieving in subjects that were mentally stimulating. I was impatient with drill and routine, questioned authority, and found it necessary to respect teachers before I could learn from them.

At school and at work: I am a conceptual and independent thinker. For me, work is play. I am drawn to constant challenges, and live to develop models, explore ideas, or build systems to satisfy my need to deal with the innovative. Once I have perfected an idea, I prefer to move on, leaving the project to be maintained and supported by others.

In relationships: I prefer to let my head rule my heart. I dislike repetition, so it is difficult for me to continuously express feelings. I believe that once feelings are stated, they are obvious to a partner. I am uneasy when my emotions control me; I want to establish a relationship and leave it to maintain itself.

(This resource is taken from Don Lowry's *True Colors* [Laguna Beach, CA: Communication Companies, International]. All rights reserved. Used with permission.)

"Our Deepest Fear"

Our deepest fear is not that we are inadequate.
Our deepest fear is that we are powerful beyond measure.
It is our light, not our darkness that most frightens us.
We ask ourselves, who am I to be brilliant, gorgeous, talented, fabulous?
Actually, who are you *not* to be?
You are a child of God.
Your playing small does not serve the world.
There is nothing enlightened about shrinking so that other people won't feel insecure around you.
We are all meant to shine, as children do.
We were born to make manifest the glory of God that is within us.
It is not just in some of us; it is in everyone.
And as we let our own light shine,
we unconsciously give other people permission to do the same.
As we are liberated from our own fear,
our presence automatically liberates others.

(Marianne Williamson, *A Return to Love: Reflections on the Principles of "A Course in Miracles,"* [New York: Harper Collins, 1992], chapter 7, section 3, at *www.skdesigns.com/internet/articles/quotes/williamson.html,* accesssed May 6, 2003.)

Color Prayer

Leader: Just as God promised Moses that he would be with him, so God walks with each of us. Our response to the petitions will be: God, you are near; let me call on you.

Blue reader: God, help us all to be more understanding, more patient, more nurturing, more spiritual. May we become more and more conscious that these gifts come from you. We pray . . .

Gold reader: God, help us to be strong, confident, ambitious, and loyal. We trust that you have made us good, and we believe that we are capable of great things in our lives—if we live up to the challenges of our giftedness. We pray . . .

Orange reader: God, help us to stay focused, to be serious about those things that need our attention, to be disciplined in our lives, and to be fair in our decisions. May the knowledge that we have and the intelligence that you have given us be used for the good of all. We pray . . .

Green reader: God, help each of us to face life with humor and spontaneity. May we live lives that are generous, exciting, creative, and full of joy. Help us to see with new eyes the wonders of this world that you created—and may our lives bring joy to those around us. We pray . . .

Reader 1: "Our Deepest Fear," by Marianne Williamson, from resource 2

Leader: Let us bow our heads and pray together:

> We ask you, heavenly Father, to give us the courage we need to be all you have called us to be. We ask you to walk with us as we discover ourselves in the days, months, and years ahead. We ask this through Christ, our model and friend. Amen.

4 The Importance of Community

AT A GLANCE

Study It

Core Session:
Christian Community
(60 minutes)
- Are We Ever Alone?
  (20 minutes)
- Scripture and Tradition Reflection
  (40 minutes)

Pray It
- Body of Christ
  (10 minutes)

Live It
- Being the Body of Christ
- Global interdependence

Overview

As Christians we recognize the importance of community. Throughout the sacred Scriptures, God reveals the importance of each individual that makes up the community, and the importance of the community as a whole. Paul uses the image of the Body of Christ to help the early Christian community recognize their interdependence as they preach the Gospel. This session invites the participants to examine the importance of Christian community and the ways they are called to establish and participate in community.

Outcomes

- The participants will recognize their interdependence.
- The participants will explore images of community within the Scriptures and Church teaching.
- The participants will understand the image of the Body of Christ.

Background Reading

- *Catholic Youth Bible* article connections: "The Body of Christ" (1 Cor. 12:12–31), "We Are the Body of Christ" (Rom. 12:1–8)

Core Session: Christian Community (60 minutes)

Preparation
- Gather the following items:
  - ❏ newsprint, enough for each group of eight to have two sheets, and additional newsprint for other activities
  - ❏ markers, one for each participant
  - ❏ masking tape
  - ❏ *Catholic Youth Bible*s or other Bibles, one for each group of six
- Copy handout 2, "Scripture and Tradition." Make six copies of each "assignment," so that each group of six receives six copies of one of the assignments. If you have more than thirty people, two groups can work on the same assignment. If you have fewer than thirty people, consider making the groups smaller so that each of the assignments can be given to a group. However, groups should not have fewer than four people.
- Designate or provide a small-group facilitator for each group of six participants.
- Cut the newsprint sheets in half. The newsprint sheet should be in the landscape orientation. You will need two half-sheets of newsprint for every six participants.
- Gather in a space that will allow each small group to work together, either around a table or on the floor, allowing space on which to write.

Are We Ever Alone? (20 minutes)

1. Welcome the participants. Divide them into groups of eight. Give each group a sheet of newsprint and a marker, and introduce the activity with these comments:
- Each group has a piece of newsprint and a marker. Working as a team, you will need to brainstorm a list of activities that you do alone—in other words, things you do not need anyone else's help to accomplish.

Give the groups about 3 minutes to work.

2. Collect the newsprint sheets from each group, and then redistribute them so that each group gets another group's newsprint sheet. Give each group a new sheet of newsprint. Give the participants the following instructions:

- You were asked to brainstorm activities you do alone, but now I am going to ask you to figure out all the other people who are involved in the activities you believe you do alone.
- Using the newsprint from the other group, choose one of their activities. At the top of the new sheet of newsprint, write the name of the activity you have chosen and then make a list of all the people or companies who are connected to the activity you chose. For instance, if sleeping is on your list, you might want to consider the following questions: Who made the bed? Who paid for the bed? Who made the sheets? From where did the bed, sheets, pajamas, and blanket come? Who picked the cotton? Who cut the lumber? Try to create a list of all the people, places, and companies that play a role in the activity you chose.
- You will have to work fast, because you have only 3 minutes to accomplish your task.

3. When the groups have completed their work, invite everyone back to a common area. Using masking tape, post each of the newsprint sheets a few feet from each other on a wall. Give each participant a marker. Give the following directions to the participants:

- Each group had a chance to work on a list—but I still think that additional people, places, or companies have been missed.
- In groups of three, go up to each posted sheet of newsprint, read what is on the list, and then add to it if you can think of any additions.
- Find two other people to work with, and when I say go, get to work. You will have only 4 minutes to work.

Allow some time for everyone to get into their groups of three. Make sure no one is left out of this activity. When everyone is ready, say go.

4. Gather the participants into a large group, and ask:
- What does this activity tell you?
- When people use the word *independent,* do you think they really are able to do something independently?
- What do you think is meant by *interdependence?* What are some examples?

5. Conclude this activity with the following comments:
- The famous poet John Donne once said, "No man is an island, entire of itself; every man is a piece of the continent" (*Devotions Upon Emergent Occasions,* Meditation XVII). He was acknowledging that it is impossible for us to think that we live our lives outside the influence of other people. Satellites, television, and the Internet all contribute to a global sense of community. In fact, the name "World Wide Web" is a great description of how computers have joined us with others.
- The activity was a fun way to get us in touch with all the ways we depend on others. What is true in our "regular" life is also true in our faith life. We

depend on one another, and are connected to one another through our faith in Jesus Christ and our participation in the Catholic Church.
- Next, we will spend some time exploring what it means to be a community within our faith Tradition. We are going to look at the Scriptures and some Church documents to help us do that.

Scripture and Tradition Reflection (40 minutes)

1. To begin the activity, divide the participants into groups of six. Give each group a Bible and six copies of one of the assignments from handout 2, "Scripture and Tradition," as well as two half-sheets of newsprint and a marker. Ask a small-group facilitator to join each group. Introduce the activity with the following words:

- Each group has received an assignment. Your job is to do two things. First, read the Scripture passage you have been assigned and talk about the question on the handout. After discussing the question, proceed to the directions for using the newsprint. When you have finished the Scripture activity, read the Church Tradition quotation and talk about the question that is posed. Then proceed to the Tradition activity.

If necessary, use one of the assignments as an example to further clarify the directions. Give the groups about 15 minutes to work, keeping an eye on each group's progress. It might be necessary to extend the time.

2. When they are finished, ask each group to present their newsprint sheets, in the order of the assignments (beginning at assignment 1) to the rest of the participants. After all groups have presented, post the newsprint sheets on the wall where everyone can see them.

3. Now ask the participants, as a whole, if they can unscramble the letters into a word or phrase. They will be able to spell out "Body of Christ" with the newsprint sheets.

4. From the newsprint letters, outline the following ideas about community, drawing on the work the groups have presented:
- B – We are *bound* together as community.
- O – We are *obliged* to help one another—especially those who are most in need.
- D – We are *dependent* on one another.
- Y – *Youth* have an important role in building community.
- O – We are all *one*, throughout the world, joined together by God.
- F – Community demands *forgiveness* and love.
- C – Church is *community*, and without community, there is no Church.
- H – Community helps us to live *holy* lives.
- R – We have a *right* (and a duty) to share our gifts for the good of others.
- I – We are *interdependent*—we need other's gifts and they need ours.

- S – We are all called to *service* within the parish community.
- T – We are called to *teach* about Jesus through our words and actions.

5. End with the following closing thoughts:

- We have looked at the ways our Church teaches about community. In addition to the sacred Scriptures and our Tradition (including the official writings of the Church, which we have seen), there is a third necessary element of Church—the Christian community.
- The role of the community within our Catholic faith stands right beside the Scriptures and Tradition.
- As we continue on our spiritual journeys, we will find that the struggles, wisdom, religious practices, and life experiences of those around us can do much to help us grow in faith.
- If we rely only on our own experience of God in our lives, we will be missing a big piece of the puzzle. As Paul said, "The eye cannot say to the hand, 'I have no need of you'" (1 Cor. 12:21). We need one another to know and understand God, and others need us to play our part in the Body of Christ.
- Let us gather for prayer, remembering that we are called to community, and that we share in community in a special way when we pray together.

Pray It

Body of Christ (10 minutes)

Preparation
- Gather the following items:
  - ❏ a *Catholic Youth Bible* or other Bible
  - ❏ *Spirit & Song* books, or another hymnal of your choosing, one for each participant
- Invite a participant to proclaim 1 Cor. 12:12–21.
- Choose opening and closing songs, to be sung by the participants. Suggestions follow under *"Spirit & Song* Connections."

1. Begin by inviting the participants to prepare for prayer with a moment of silence, and then invite the participants to sing the opening song.

2. Invite the designated reader to come forward to proclaim the Scripture passage. Allow a few moments of silence to follow.

Spirit & Song connections

- ◆ "Somos el Cuerpo de Cristo/We Are the Body of Christ," by Jaime Cortez
- ◆ "We Are One Body," by Dana Scallon
- ◆ "We Are God's People," by Jeffrey Roscoe

3. Offer the following reflection:

- "Scripture uses the expression the 'Body of Christ' to mean three things: *Jesus,* the historical person who walked the earth for thirty-three years; the *Eucharist,* which is the physical presence of God among us; and the *body of believers,* which is also the real presence. To say the word "Christ" is to refer, at one and the same time, to Jesus, the Eucharist, and the community of faith.

    "We are the Body of Christ. This is not an exaggeration, nor a metaphor. . . .

    "If it is true that we are the Body of Christ, and it is, then God's presence in the world today depends very much upon us. We have to keep God present in the world in the same way as Jesus did. We have to become, as Teresa of Ávila so simply put it, God's physical hands, feet, mouthpiece, and heart in this world." (Ronald Rolheiser, *The Holy Longing,* pp. 79–80)

4. Invite all the participants to offer each other a sign of peace in a unique way by saying, "You are important to me" (instead of "Peace be with you") to all the participants.

5. Conclude by inviting the participants to sing the closing song.

Options and Actions

- **Being the Body of Christ.** Invite the participants to think about something they enjoy doing or are good at. Invite them to find a new way to use their gifts within the community (including their family and the parish) for the good of others. They might consider mentoring a younger person, volunteering, extending friendship or a listening ear, and other ideas.
- **Global interdependence.** As a group, consider participating in Operation Ricebowl (contact Catholic Relief Services, *www.catholicrelief.org,* for free supplies) or purchasing an animal through Heifer International *(www.heiferproject.org)* that will be given to a poor family.

Family connections

Invite the participants to think about all the different roles the members of their families play. Who earns money? Who washes clothes? Who does the grocery shopping? Who reads a book to a small child? Invite families to talk about the importance that each person plays in the family and how each has a special role. They may all be different, but without each person, the family would be different (and probably not as strong).

Media connections

- *Entertaining Angels: The Dorothy Day Story* (Warner Studios, 112 minutes, 1996, rated PG-13)
- *The Mission* (Warner Studios, 125 minutes, 1986, rated PG)
- The Catholic Campaign for Human Development's Web site *(www.usccb.org/cchd)* includes a tour of the face of poverty *(www.povertyusa.org).* Invite the young people to take the tour and reflect on the ways in which they could be a part of the solution to poverty in the world today.

Scripture and Tradition

Assignment 1

1. Read Acts of the Apostles 2:42–47.

2. Talk about the following question: Why did they hold "all things in common"? (This means that no one had individual property; all was shared within the community.)

3. On one of the sheets of newsprint, make a large B, filling the page with it. In and around the B, write down all the things that bond you with one another and with other Catholics.

4. Read the following excerpt:

   > The challenge of being transformed into a holy person is not undertaken alone but within a faith community. . . . Within the community, we develop our potential, foster our talents, form our identity, and respond to the many challenges of being holy men and women. (*Sons and Daughters of the Light: A Pastoral Plan for Ministry with Young Adults,* by the United States Conference of Catholic Bishops [USCCB]

   [Washington, DC: USCCB, 1997], page 19. Copyright © 1996 by the USCCB. All rights reserved. Found at *www.usccb.org/laity/ygadult/toc.htm,* accessed May 30, 2003.)

5. Talk about the following question: Who do you know within this Catholic community or beyond that is a holy person?

6. On one of the sheets of newsprint, make a large H, filling the page with it. In and around the H, write down some things you can do to help you to be holy (examples include private prayer, social-justice projects, and the Eucharist).

Assignment 2

1. Read John 17:17–21.

2. Talk about the following question: Who taught you about the Catholic faith?

3. On one of the sheets of newsprint, make a large T, filling the page with it. In and around the T, write down the places and people that teach you about Jesus through word and example.

4. Read the following excerpt:

   > Community is not only an abstract principle but also a concrete reality lived each day at home, on campus, within society, and in organizations, movements, and parishes.
   >
   > Community is God's promise to those who have accepted the gracious invitation to live the Gospel and to be lights for the world. (*Sons and Daughters of the Light: A Pastoral Plan for Ministry with Young Adults,* by the United States Conference of Catholic Bishops

   [USCCB] [Washington, DC: USCCB, 1997], page 19. Copyright © 1996 by the USCCB. All rights reserved. Found at *www.usccb.org/laity/ygadult/toc.htm,* accessed May 30, 2003.)

5. Talk about the following question: What have you learned about community through your family (immediate and extended family, and other people whom you count as family)?

6. On one of the sheets of newsprint, make a large Y, filling the page with it. In and around the Y, write down some things that you, as young people, can do to help build community in your family, school, and parish.

Assignment 3

1. Read Acts of the Apostles 4:32–35.

2. Talk about the following question: Why did the early Christians give everything they had to the Apostles for distribution to those who were in need?

3. On one of the sheets of newsprint, make a large D, filling the page with it. In and around the D, write down some things you need for which you depend on others.

4. Read the following excerpt:

   > The obligation to provide justice for all means that the poor have the single most urgent economic claim on the conscience of the nation. . . . As individuals and as a nation, therefore, we are called to make a fundamental "option for the poor."[1] The obligation to evaluate social and economic activity from the viewpoint of the poor and the powerless arises from the radical command to love one's neighbor as one's self. Those who are marginalized and whose rights are denied have privileged claims if society is to provide justice for *all*. This obligation is deeply rooted in Christian belief. As Paul VI stated: "In teaching us charity, the Gospel instructs us in the preferential respect due to the poor and the special situation they have in society: the more fortunate should renounce some of their rights so as to place their goods more generously at the service of others."[2]

   1. On the recent use of this term see: Congregation for the Doctrine of the Faith, "Instruction on Christian Freedom and Liberation," 46–50, 66–68; "Evangelization in Latin America's Present and Future," Final Document of the Third General Conference of the Latin American Episcopate (Puebla, Mexico, January 27–February 13, 1979), esp. part VI, ch. 1, "A Preferential Option for the Poor," in J. Eagleson and P. Scharper, eds, "Puebla and Beyond" (Maryknoll, NY: Orbis Books, 1979), 264–267; Donald Dorr, "Option for the Poor: A Hundred Years of Vatican Social Teaching" (Dublin: Gill and Macmillan/Maryknoll, NY: Orbis Books, 1983).
   2. Octogesima Adveniens, 23.

   (*Economic Justice for All: Pastoral Letter on Catholic Social Teaching and the U.S. Economy*, by the United States Conference of Catholic Bishops [USCCB] [Washington, DC: USCCB, 1986], numbers 86–87. Copyright © 1986 by the USCCB. All rights reserved. Found at *www.osjspm.org/cst/eja.htm*, accessed May 30, 2003.)

5. Talk about the following question: What is the meaning of the last sentence of the preceding quote—specifically to those who live in the United States?

6. On one of the sheets of newsprint, make a large O, filling the page with it. In and around the O, write down reasons we are obliged to share our wealth (material, spiritual, other) with all people.

Assignment 4

1. Read Romans 12:1–8.

2. Talk about the following question: The Apostle Paul uses the image of the Body of Christ to describe the Church and its members. Why?

3. On one of the sheets of newsprint, make a large S, filling the page with it. In and around the S, write down all the different ways you can serve within the parish community, listing the ministries (titles, jobs, actions) of the parish.

4. Read the following excerpt:

   From the acceptance of these charisms [unique talents or spiritual gifts], including those which are more elementary, there arise for each believer the right and duty to use them in the Church and in the world for the good of [humankind] and the building up of the Church.

   (Vatican Council II, *Decree on the Apostolate of the Laity,* 1965, number 3, at www.vatican.va/archive/hist_councils/ii_vatican_council/documents/vat-ii_decree_19651118_apostolicam-actuositatem_en.html, accessed May 14, 2003)

5. Talk about the following question: Why do the bishops say we have both a *right* and a *duty* to use our gifts within the Church and the world?

6. On one of the sheets of newsprint, make a large R, filling the page with it. In and around the R, write down some of the gifts (talents, interests, ideas) you have a right to share to make the world a better place.

Assignment 5

1. Read 1 Corinthians 12:12–21.

2. Talk about the following question: Why do humans have such a strong need for one another? (Why can't we say, "I don't need you"?)

3. On one of the sheets of newsprint, make a large I, filling the page with it. In and around the I, write down some ways this parish is interdependent (in other words, everyone has something to offer, but also needs the gifts of others).

4. Read the following excerpt:

   > The Kingdom aims at transforming human relationships; it grows gradually as people slowly learn to love, forgive, and serve one another.

   (John Paul II, *On the Permanent Validity of the Church's Missionary Mandate,* 1990, number 15, at *www.vatican.va/holy_father/john_paul_ii/encyclicals/documents/ hf_jp-ii_enc_07121990_redemptoris-missio_en.html,* accessed May 14, 2003)

5. Talk about the following question: Why are love and forgiveness tied together in this teaching?

6. On one of the sheets of newsprint, make a large F, filling the page with it. In and around the F, write down some reasons that forgiveness within communities is so important.

Assignment 6

1. Read Ephesians 4:1–7.

2. Talk about the following question: Paul is trying to tell the disciples that everyone comes from the same God—that we are all one. Does it seem like that is an important message for today's world? Why?

3. On one of the sheets of newsprint, make a large O, filling the page with it. In and around the O, write down some ways the world would be different if it were "one"—without the divisions that seem to exist among people.

4. Read the following excerpt:

   > Now the laity are called in a special way to make the Church present and operative in those places and circumstances where only through them can it become the salt of the earth. Thus every lay [person], in virtue of the very gifts bestowed upon him, is at the same time a witness and a living instrument of the mission of the Church itself "according to the measure of Christ's bestowal" (Ephesians 4:7).

   (Vatican Council II, *Dogmatic Constitution on the Church [Lumen Gentium]*, 1964, number 33, at *www.vatican.va/archive/hist_councils/ii_vatican_council/documents/ vat-ii_const_19641121_ lumen-gentium_en.html,* accessed May 14, 2003)

5. Talk about the following question: Where are some places you can "make the Church present" (meaning, "be the hands and feet of Christ")?

6. On one of the sheets of newsprint, make a large C, filling the page with it. In and around the C, write down some ways this Catholic parish is, or could be, a strong Christian community.

5 Making Friends

AT A GLANCE

Study It

Core Session:
The Friendship Experiment
(45 minutes)

- Data: The Qualities of a Good Friend (10 minutes)
- Research: How *You* Can Be a Good Friend (20 minutes)
- Findings: The Friendship Journal (15 minutes)

Session Extensions

- Friendship in Action (15 minutes)
- Circle of Friends (15 minutes)

Pray It

- God and Friends (10 minutes)

Overview

As young people begin to feel the natural need to move outside their family for self-definition, friends play an important role in answering the question, Who am I? As adults we can help young people recognize the importance of being a good friend and surrounding themselves with good people. Jesus is a model for us as we look at the characteristics of friendship because he surrounded himself with friends throughout his life. This session will help young people take a closer look at the friends they have, the friends they are seeking, and the type of friend they wish to be.

Outcomes

- The participants will be able to identify the qualities of a good friend.
- The participants will be able to reflect on their own friendships and the ways they are a good friend to others.
- The participants will pray for and with their friends.

Background Reading

- Scriptural connections: Luke 11:5–8 (providing for a friend), John 11:1–44 (the raising of Lazarus), John 15:12–17 (no greater love)
- *Catholic Youth Bible* article connections: "Friends Forever" (1 Sam., chap. 20), "Friends" (Sir. 6:5–17), "Friendship" (Phil. 1:3–11)

Core Session:
The Friendship Experiment (45 minutes)

Preparation
- Gather the following items:
  - ❑ two large sheets of newsprint
  - ❑ handout 3, "Friendship Journal," one for each participant
  - ❑ pens, one for each participant
  - ❑ a CD player and a CD of reflective music
- If your group is no larger than thirty people, you can do this activity with the whole group. If your group is larger than thirty, you will want to divide into two or more groups, depending on your overall number of participants.

Data: The Qualities of a Good Friend (10 minutes)

1. Gather the participants into a large group. Introduce the session with these words:
- Today we will be looking more closely at friendship: what makes a good friendship, how to be a good friend, how to choose good friends, and how to put friendship into action.

2. Invite the participants to call out the qualities of a good friend. You will want to note them on newsprint. Some ideas include trustworthy, encouraging, honest, loyal, respectful, and spiritual.

3. Ask the participants which of the qualities listed are nonnegotiable, meaning that without that particular quality, one could not be considered a good friend.

You might want to start by asking them to eliminate any qualities they think are not necessary. Before something comes off the list, though, you will want to ask the whole group if they agree with the suggestion to eliminate that quality. When the group is satisfied that they have a list of non-negotiable qualities, ask the participants these questions:
- Are these realistic expectations to have of your friends? Why or why not?
- Are these realistic expectations for your friends to have of you? Why or why not?

Hopefully, the participants will think that the traits they have chosen are realistic expectations of friends. If the majority answers no, work to develop a list that is realistic. Then share with the participants the following points:
- In the best-case scenario, we—and our friends—have many of these qualities and strive to be the best friends we can be. However, we know that at some time or another, everyone makes mistakes.
- Sometimes we disappoint others when we do not live up to the expectations we have listed. That's when we are grateful that our friends accept us even when we make mistakes.
- Sometimes our friends will disappoint us. That's when we work together to continue building our friendship with each other.
- The list we have generated is a good one to keep in mind when we are being a friend to others, when we are looking to make new friends, and when we have to decide whether keeping someone as a friend is the right thing to do.

4. As a transition to the next part of the session, ask for a volunteer to read "Jesus' Imperfect Friends," from *The Catholic Youth Bible (CYB),* near Matt. 26:36–45, which reads as follows:

> Imagine that you are in the middle of a crisis and ask your best friends to stay with you while you prepare to face the situation. They all promise to be there for you. But one friend after another fails to come through, and you are left to face the trauma alone.
>
> The friends of Jesus were no different. They were well intentioned and meant to stay awake with him. But in their tiredness, they let him down.
>
> We usually think that the friends of Jesus, the Apostles in particular, were special and holy. But the friends of Jesus were human and had their own weaknesses. Even Peter, one of the greatest heroes of Christianity, lacked the courage to admit he knew Jesus, as we read in Matt. 26:69–75. Yet Jesus loved them despite their failings and even when they were disloyal.
>
> Is it easy for you to stay friends with those who let you down? Can you follow the example of Jesus?

5. Make the following comments to the participants:
- Now that we have looked at the desired qualities of a friend and heard how Jesus loved his friends in spite of their weaknesses, let's take a look at how we can be good friends to others.

TryThis

As an alternative to reading the *CYB* article, you might consider brainstorming or discussing with the participants the qualities of friendship they recognize in Jesus. Or have them conduct a Scripture search to locate a few of the Gospel stories that offer insight into the friendships that Jesus shared with such people as Peter, John, Martha and Mary, Lazarus, and so forth.

Research: How *You* Can Be a Good Friend (20 minutes)

1. Divide the participants into pairs. Then ask them to share answers to the following questions with their partner:
- When were you not a good friend to someone?
- When have you been a good friend to someone?

You will want to note that the participants do not have to share names or specific details.

Allow about 5 minutes for the sharing. If time allows, you may wish to invite one or two participants to share their answers with the whole group.

2. On a sheet of newsprint, record the responses from the participants to the following question:
- How can you be a good friend?

Rather than write the previously listed qualities of a good friend, focus on concrete ways the participants can demonstrate friendship. Some examples include staying in touch with a friend through e-mail or phone calls, spending time with a friend in a shared interest, defending a friend against gossip, getting to know a friend's family, and so on.

Once a list has been generated, you will want to point out that the collected wisdom on the two newsprint sheets (qualities of a friend and ways to be a friend) are great reminders of what we need to be and do to be a good friend.

Findings: The Friendship Journal (15 minutes)

1. Distribute a copy of handout 3, "Friendship Journal," and a pen to each participant. Ask the participants to spend about 10 minutes answering the questions that most interest them. Note that it is not necessary for the participants to answer every question, but that they should answer them on their own. You may wish to play some reflective music in the background.

2. Ask if anyone would like to share one of his or her journal reflections. Encourage the participants to regularly evaluate their friends and their friendships in an effort to keep the relationships positive and healthy.

3. Close the session by offering the following comments:
- We have taken the time to reflect on the qualities needed for good friendships and on our own actions that help us to be good friends.
- We have also taken some time to journal about our friends and ourselves. By being a good friend and cultivating friendships with people who share our values, we will develop into the people that God calls us to be.

Session Extensions

Friendship in Action (15 minutes)

1. Invite the participants to think about how hard it must be not to have any good friends. Ask one or two participants to share stories about people they know (without naming names) who don't seem to have friends or about a time in their own life when they felt friendless.

2. Invite the participants to consider their personal opportunity to be a friend to someone else—either someone who seems to need a friend or simply someone whom they do not know. Encourage them to be intentional about making a new friend in the coming weeks.

3. Ask the group to brainstorm the types of people who might need a friend. Some ideas may include people who are new at school or in the neighborhood, people they may be acquainted with at school or work but haven't taken the time to get to know well, someone who is different from them in culture, ethnicity, race, religion, and so on. Encourage them to think not only of other young people but perhaps of an elderly person or of a young child who does not have brothers or sisters.

4. Offer the following questions to help the participants design a plan for initiating a new friendship:
- How will you initiate a conversation with this person?
- How will you get to know this person's interests?
- What will you do if this person doesn't seem interested in being friends?
- How will you spend time with this person?
- How will you stay in touch with this person?

Circle of Friends (15 minutes)

Preparation
- Gather the following item:
  ❑ one ball of yarn for every seven to nine participants

1. Invite the participants to divide into small groups of seven to nine people. Ask each small group to stand in a circle facing inward. Give one person in each group a ball of yarn, and invite them toss it to another person in the circle while still holding on to the loose end. The next person holds on to a piece of the yarn and tosses it to another person in the circle. Keep doing this until each person is holding part of the "web" of yarn. The ball should end with the person who started the yarn toss.

2. Direct each group to pull firmly on their yarn to create a strong, defined web. Make these comments:
- We all live in a world where we are connected with many different people. We have our families, school communities, parish community, neighborhoods, and more. We are connected to many different people in our lives.
- Sometimes we have a large circle of friends, and sometimes it is just one or two people with whom we are closely connected. This web can represent for each of us the people in our lives (family and friends) to whom we are most closely connected.
- When each person in our web of friends and family is healthy and positive, the web is also healthy. We feel good because we can feel the support of other people, and we value the friendship that is shared among us.

3. Ask two or three people in each small group to loosen their hold on the web. Then continue with these comments:
- What happens to the shape and design when you relax your hold? The web sags in some places because the connection is not as tight as it was before.
- Sometimes people need us to support them during hard times, and the value of a web of friends and family is that we can help one another through crises, distress, or just a bad day.

4. Ask everyone to pull tight again. Then ask two people simply to drop their yarn completely and leave the circle. Again, continue with these comments:
- At times people—family and friends—just drop out of our lives, and it can be painful. Sometimes they leave completely, and other times they stop being a good friend to us, and we are left feeling hurt by the change in the relationship. It is always hard to lose touch with a friend or a member of our family.
- If we have a web of people in our lives, sometimes they can support us through that difficult time. (Ask the group to pull tight on the web again, to take up the slack caused by the two people who left.)
- Our web may not look or feel the same, but the support of the friends and family still remaining in our lives is important.
- One of the joys of our faith in God is that we always know God is there to support us. We can count on God, and we know that God is a part of the whole web of relationships.

5. Ask the participants the following questions (as they continue to hold on to the yarn). The facilitator can ask people to answer these questions out loud, or they can be used for silent reflection:
- What things can help strengthen a web of friends?
- What things can destroy friendships?
- What things can help or destroy family relationships?

Familyconnections

Provide the participants with a list of discussion questions for use at home. The questions might include: Does your family ever pray together, perhaps at meals, at bedtime, or on special occasions? Does your family attend Mass together? Do you have a special role in helping to enhance your family's relationship with God? How can your family do a better job of maintaining or developing a close relationship with God? You might even consider posting these questions on your parish Web site, or e-mailing one question per week to each family.

TryThis

You may choose to end with the simple game of having each web group race to see which one can untangle and reroll their yarn the fastest.

Mediaconnections

- Consider viewing the movie *Harry Potter and the Sorcerer's Stone* (Warner Home Video, 152 minutes, 2001, rated PG), inviting the participants to pay special attention to the friendship among the main characters. You might discuss the ways in which Harry and his friends support one another, as well as the ways in which the friendships grow and change throughout the movie.
- Check out *Toy Story* (Walt Disney Home Video, 81 minutes, 1995, rated G) and *Toy Story 2* (Disney/Pixar, 93 minutes, 1999, rated G). These movies offer good insights into friendship.
- The movie *Now and Then* (New Line Studios, 102 minutes, 1995, rated PG-13) tells the story of four friends who grow up together. The movie theme would provide a great discussion on the subject of lifelong friendships and ways to maintain them.

Spirit & Song connections

- "Lean on Me," by Bill Withers
- "Gather Your People," by Bob Hurd

---

6. Close by making the following comments:

- One of the reasons it is so important to work at being a good friend and to choose good friends is that those relationships help us throughout our lives.
- Friendships may change and people may come and go, but if we constantly work at deepening our friendships, creating new ones, and supporting others, we will find that our lives are healthier and happier.
- Of course, the same is true for the relationships that we have with our families. It is important to treat our families as well as we do our friends, and to let those relationships grow and change throughout our lives.
- Having God as a part of each of our relationships makes those relationships stronger. We can find God reflected in each and every person that we meet in life, and when we recognize that God is present in others, it makes our relationships stronger.

God and Friends (10 minutes)

Preparation

- Choose a closing song such as "Friends," by Michael W. Smith (*The First Decade, 1983–1993,* Meadowgreen Music Company [ASCAP], 1982), or another song with a friendship theme.
- Invite a young person or an adult to share a brief reflection on how God is part of her or his friendships.

1. Gather the young people into a prayerful space or atmosphere. Ask everyone to be quiet, pausing for perhaps 30 seconds of silence, and then invite the participants to think about how God is a part of their relationships with family and friends. If possible, have a young person or an adult share a brief reflection on how God is an important part of his or her friendships.

2. Ask each person to think about someone with whom they feel comfortable sharing their faith journey. Invite the participants to name that person aloud. Then offer the following prayer:

- We thank you, God, for the people that you have given us to help us know and love you more fully. We ask you to bless each of the individuals we have named. May they continue to grow in their faith, may they help us to do the same, and may the bond of faith we share continue to help us grow together in friendship and love.

3. Conclude the prayer by playing the closing song you have chosen.

Friendship Journal

Spend some time journaling about the following questions. You do not need to answer each question. Concentrate on the questions that interest you the most.

- Who are the people (friends or acquaintances) that you would most want to be like?

- What do you like most about your friend(s)?

- What bothers you about your friend(s)?

- What makes you a good friend?

- What do you need to work on to be a better friend?

- Is it easy to talk to your friends about the things that are most important to you, including your faith?

- How have your friendships changed over the years?

- Is it easy for you to make friends? If not, what seems to make it difficult?

- Is it easy for you to keep friendships going? If not, what seems to cause problems?

- Do you have friends of different ages? races? religions? ethnic backgrounds? genders?

- Do you have some friends of whom your parents don't approve? Do you know why they don't approve of them?

- What have you learned through your friendships?

Music and Me

AT A GLANCE

Study It

Core Session: Tuning In (60 minutes)
- My Taste in Music (20 minutes)
- Personal Song Selections (40 minutes)

Session Extensions
- Be Not Afraid . . . Understanding Church Music (20 minutes)
- Musical Styles and Their Cultural Stereotypes (20 minutes)

Pray It
- Praying Through Our Music (10 minutes)

Live It
- Broaden your horizons
- Share your talent

Overview

Today, as in the past, many young people define themselves by the music they listen to and the artists they like. Music also helps them express themselves—they use the lyrics of a favorite song to help put into words their emotions or their life experiences. Many times music helps youth express their relationship with God. This session invites the participants to get to know one another through listening to and experiencing with their peers the music they most enjoy. The participants will be challenged to experience different styles of music, and to recognize that music can help to celebrate the differences among people.

Outcomes

- The participants will become better acquainted with their peers and the adults who participate.
- The participants will be invited to be open-minded about different musical styles—and different people.
- The participants will discuss how music affects them and reflects their mood, their actions, and their dress.

Background Reading

- *Catholic Youth Bible* article connections: "Miriam Leads the People in Praise" (Exod. 15:1–21), "Judith Leads the Prayer-Song" (Jth. 16:1–20), "Have You Sung This Before?" (Ps. 91)

Core Session: Tuning In (60 minutes)

Preparation
- Gather the following items:
  - ❏ a CD or cassette player
  - ❏ blank sheets of paper, one for each participant
  - ❏ pens or markers, one for each participant
  - ❏ masking tape
  - ❏ index cards, one for each participant
  - ❏ boxes, baskets, or bags (one for each style of music to which you plan to have your group listen)
- Label each box, basket, or bag with the name of one musical style, for example, rap, classical, heavy metal, country, reggae, and so on.
- Before the session, ask the participants (both youths and adults, if desired) to bring a recording—on CD or cassette—of one of their favorite songs. Ask the participants to choose a song they really connect with, either because of the music or the words. If possible, they should bring the song lyrics with them. Be sure the participants know the parameters of an appropriate song for this session.
- The ideas on resource 3, "Considering Your Music," should be made into visual aids. You might consider a PowerPoint presentation, posters, overheads, "bumper stickers," or a handout.

My Taste in Music (20 minutes)

1. Explain to the group that this session will focus on different musical styles and tastes. Make the following points:
- There are many different musical styles, and those differences should be celebrated among people.
- We can learn something new about people by understanding the types of music they enjoy and the songs that are most meaningful to them.
- We will have a chance to get to know one another better by finding out more about the musical tastes of the members of our group and by sharing with one another some of the music that is most important to each of us.
- It is important that we don't ridicule other people's musical tastes. What people like to listen to is a reflection of who they are—and that is sacred.

2. Give each participant a sheet of paper and a pen or marker. Proceed through the following instructions, allowing time for the participants to complete each task before introducing the next one. You might consider demonstrating the instructions for the group on a chalkboard or a sheet of newsprint. The paper should be used in landscape format.
- In the middle of the paper, ask each participant to write his or her name. Instruct the participants to write the name of the artist and the song they have brought with them in the top left-hand corner of the paper.
- In the bottom right-hand corner of the paper, ask them to write the style of music they most enjoy (rap, reggae, classical, rock and roll, and so forth).
- In the top right-hand corner of the paper, ask the participants to write the name of a favorite CD, something other than the one they brought with them.
- Then ask the participants to write the style of music they like least in the bottom left-hand corner of their paper.
- Now instruct everyone to write the names of five of their favorite artists in the area above their name.
- In the area below their name, have the participants list five words that describe what they like about music. For example, they might like music to be loud, to be energized, to have meaningful words, to be easy to accompany with air guitar, and so on.

3. Give each of the participants a piece of masking tape, and ask them to tape the piece of paper to their shirt (like an oversized nametag).

4. Invite the participants to mingle throughout the room, and to try to make sure they look at everyone's paper. Tell them that they should also be looking for similarities and differences between themselves and others. Allow about 3 to 5 minutes for this mingling, depending on the size of the group.

5. Ask each person to find one other person in the group who seems to have musical tastes different from their own. Once they locate a partner, they should find a place in the room to sit down together.

6. Ask each pair to talk about their musical tastes by discussing the information they have listed on their sheets of paper. Allow a few minutes for this one-on-one sharing.

7. Ask for a few participants to share with the entire group something they have learned about someone else in the group. Then share the following comments:
- We can gain insights about others by learning more about their musical tastes. We can discover a point of connection with someone when we

share a love for a song or an artist. We can also discover a topic for conversation when we share our reaction to a concert we have attended, the words to our favorite song, or what we know about our favorite artists.
- We can gain insights about a person by listening to the types of music they enjoy or the particular songs they call their favorites. Today we want to listen to some of the music that you brought with you.

Personal Song Selections (40 minutes)

1. If the group as a whole is larger than ten people, you will want to limit the number of songs you play during this session. To ensure that everyone's song is played, you might choose to play some of the songs at different gatherings throughout the year, especially if the group meets on a regular basis. To choose which songs will be played (in larger groups), give each participant an index card and ask them to write their name, the style of music (rap, classical, and so forth) of their song, and the name of the song and artist they have chosen. Ask the participants to put their index cards in the box, basket, or bag that is labeled with the corresponding type of music.

2. Inform the participants that they are going to have the chance to listen to some of the selections they have chosen—at least one from each of the types of music represented in the group. Remind the participants to listen with an open mind.

3. One at a time, choose a song from each of the containers. Announce the name of the song, the kind of music it is, and who chose the song. Give the person an opportunity to explain why the song is important to her or him. After each song, discuss the following questions with the participants:
- What was your experience of the song (emotional reactions, memories, and so forth)?
- Did the song make you think about anything in particular?
- What does this song say about our culture or our faith?

You will want to repeat this step for each song you have chosen to play.

4. After listening to the different musical selections, invite the participants to discuss the following questions. If your group is larger than twenty-five people, you may wish to do this in small groups of about eight.
- Does music reflect or affect our personality? our mood? our beliefs? our culture? How so?
- What are some similarities among the songs that you heard?
- Why do you think we each respond differently to different kinds of music?

5. Make the following comments:

- We have spent most of our time talking about music we enjoy and about being open to other people and their favorite musical styles and tastes. (Be sure to include the key points mentioned by the participants during the large-group discussion.)
- It is also important to take a moment to think about the music we listen to from the perspective of our faith, and with attention to the things that will help us live happy and healthy lives.

6. Present the information found on resource 3, "Considering Your Music." This presentation can be as simple as reading through the material, or can be done creatively through skits, commercials, posters, and so on. After the material is presented, invite the participants to comment on the ideas represented. You might consider asking them these questions:
- What makes sense about these "words of wisdom"?
- What challenges do they present to you?
- What would you add or delete from these ideas? Why?

Session Extensions

Be Not Afraid . . . Understanding Church Music (20 minutes)

Preparation
- Gather the following items:
    - ❑ copies of your church hymnal or songbook, one for each pair of participants
    - ❑ *Catholic Youth Bible*s or other Bibles, one for each pair of or group of three participants
- Select songs commonly used by your parish at liturgies. Check to see if a Scripture reference is noted for the particular song. If a Scripture reference is not noted for a particular song, read through the lyrics and determine the primary faith theme(s) expressed in the song.
- Review the outline and be prepared to help the participants answer questions, or suggest ideas.

1. Introduce the session with these or similar comments:
- As with any type of music, Church music appeals to people in different ways. Some people love the sound of the organ playing and the choir singing. Some people love the sound of guitars and drums at Church. Others wish that the music were mostly quiet and meditative, and still others would like to be able to clap to every song they sing in Church. One musical style will not suit everyone. Some young people "tune out" Church music, claiming that it is boring, out of touch, slow, and not relevant. And other young people really appreciate liturgical music.

TryThis

Conduct this activity in a gender-specific group, and discuss how contemporary music influences the way we think about and treat females and males. The participants should be able to name negative images (gender stereotypes) that appear in songs and music videos. Ask them how influenced they think they are by these words and images.

- Today we will look at familiar songs we use during our parish's Masses and prayer services, to find out more about what they are trying to tell us about God. We will explore what the authors of the songs are trying to communicate.

2. Divide the participants into pairs or groups of three. Provide each pair or group with a copy of the chosen hymnal and a Bible. Assign a different hymn to each small group. Each song will be based either on a Scripture passage or a belief of the Church. Ask each pair or group to determine if the assigned song is based on a Scripture passage. If so, they should locate the Scripture passage in their Bible. If not, have the group work together to determine what belief of the Church the song is reflecting.

3. If the song has a Scripture reference, the group should discuss (after reading the Scripture passage) the following questions:
- What do the Scripture passage and the song say about God, Jesus, the Church, or faith?
- Does the song do a good job of communicating the message of the Scripture passage? Why or why not?
- Is the song appealing to you? Why or why not?

If the song is not based on a Scripture passage, the participants should discuss the following questions:
- What does this song say about God, Jesus, the Church, or faith?
- Does this song do a good job of communicating a message? Why or why not?
- Is the song appealing to you? Why or why not?

4. If time permits, allow each pair or group to share their findings with the large group.

5. Close with the following comments:
- People often like a song because the words of the song connect to an experience or a feeling they have had. Church music should also connect us to scriptural images, experiences of God, expressions of faith, or new insights and understandings about our faith.
- Sometimes we don't find the hymns meaningful because we haven't taken the time to think about the music, to really listen to the ideas expressed in them. Other times the music and lyrics seem to speak to us directly. This is not unlike the other kinds of music we all listen to on a regular basis.
- Sometimes we don't connect to a particular song that might be someone else's favorite simply because we haven't yet experienced God in the way that is being expressed in the song. Or, our interpretation of that song might be different from another person's interpretation.

Try This

Instead of using hymns, ask the participants to look at the words of contemporary Christian music and discuss the questions in step 3. This activity might help young people recognize that not all Christian music expresses Catholic beliefs. Christian music often has a theological underpinning that is distinct from Catholic theology. Leaders of the activity should be prepared to help the young people explore the faith themes in the music they have selected and to comment on the differences between other Christian denominations' understandings of God and Catholic theology.

- Sometimes we struggle to appreciate a hymn because the style of music is different from what we enjoy listening to.
- Sometimes we love a hymn because the sound of it or the words of the song touch us in a meaningful way, regardless of whether it is our regular style of music or not.
- Every day new Church music is being written, and every day we can experience God in new ways. In the coming weeks, remain open to the possibilities of learning by listening carefully to the music you sing at Mass. Give careful attention to the prayers of the community during Mass. Really think about your own prayers. Take some time with the music you listen to at home. You just may come to a new understanding and a new experience of God.

Musical Styles and Their Cultural Stereotypes (20 minutes)

Preparation
- Gather the following items:
  - ❑ newsprint and markers

1. Invite the participants to brainstorm a list of musical styles (rock, rap, jazz, reggae, classical, new age, and so on). List these styles on newsprint as they are called out.

2. Discuss the following questions:
- Who is stereotypically associated with each of these styles of music?
- How do those stereotypes get started?
- When you think about any of the musical styles, do you think that the people associated with that musical style are portrayed negatively or positively? (For example, are country music artists thought of as better people than rap music artists?)
- How do you define what you like and dislike with regard to musical style?

3. End the discussion by reminding the participants that though many different musical styles exist, there are even more "styles" of people, people from different backgrounds and with different values and ideas. Learning to respect others (and their musical styles) is important. It is especially important if we are truly Christian and believe that God created all people in his image and likeness. When we do not value or respect people who are different from us, we are turning our back on God.

Spirit & Song connections

- "Malo, Malo, Thanks Be to God," by Jesse Manibusan
- "How Can I Keep from Singing," attributed to Robert Lowry
- "Everybody Sing Alleluia," by Tony Melendez and Augie Leal

Praying Through Our Music (10 minutes)

Preparation
- Gather the following items:
  - ❑ a *Catholic Youth Bible* or other Bible
  - ❑ a candle
  - ❑ a small table (with a cloth covering, if possible)
- Invite a participant to proclaim Ps. 150.
- Invite a participant to read the reflection in step 7.
- Choose an appropriate closing song. Possible options can be found in "*Spirit & Song* Connections."

   1. Invite the participants to gather in groups of about five people. Each person should have a copy of the song they used in the core session and the lyrics to that song.

   2. Ask each group to look through the words of each of the songs and see if they think any phrases, sentences, words, or ideas conveyed in the song speak about God, our relationship to God, or our Catholic faith. Remind the participants, if necessary, that love, friendship, loyalty, and so forth, are reflections of the love that God has for us. The words they are choosing don't have to be explicitly religious. Once a lyric is selected, the group should choose one person from their group who will speak their lyric aloud during prayer.

   This person should be reminded to hold on to the lyrics, written on the CD liner, during the prayer service, because they will be placing the CDs on the prayer table. (Note: It is possible that a group will not be able to find anything appropriate in the lyrics of the songs they have chosen. If that is the case, they should be allowed to pass and not present a prayer.)

   3. When each of the groups has chosen a lyric, invite the participants to gather in the prayer space.

   4. Begin with the following prayer:

- Gracious and loving God, we thank you for the gift of music in our world. We thank you for the songs that inspire us, for the music that gets us dancing, for the times when a lyric touches our heart, and for the way we can feel while listening to it. We thank you for the people who have been gifted with remarkable talent to play, compose, and sing. We thank you for marching bands, CD Walkmans, piano teachers, African drums, bell choirs, children singing with Elmo, and all the ways that music enters our lives. We thank you for our diverse musical tastes and for the gift of song in our lives.

5. Invite each person to place their CD or cassette tape on the prayer table. They should do this quietly and one at a time.

6. Ask the team member to come forward and proclaim the Scripture passage. Allow a few moments of silence to follow.

7. Then invite the volunteer reader to come forward and share the following reflection:

> Praise God with clarinet and saxophone;
> > praise God with flute and oboe!
> Praise God with French horn and tuba;
> > praise God with marimba and xylophone!
> Praise God with guitar and fiddle;
> > praise God with banjo and ukulele!
> Praise God with bagpipe and accordion;
> > praise God with piano and calliope!
> Praise God with steel drum and harmonica;
> > praise God with bongo and maracas!
> Praise God with soaring classical music;
> > praise God with mellow blues, and tango!
> Praise God with reggae and rap;
> > praise God with jazz and rock!
> Praise God with square dancing and line dancing;
> > praise God with polka and waltz!
> Let everyone who has breath and hands and feet and voices—
> > sopranos, altos, tenors, and basses—
> > praise the Lord!
> ("Psalm 150, Part 2," in *The Catholic Youth Bible,* near Psalm 150)

8. Continue by sharing the following prayer:
- God, Creator of all good things, we know we can find you anywhere in our world. We have specifically looked for you in the music that we listen to all the time, and we have found you there. We hear about you in these words . . .

Invite each of the groups to share the lyrics they have chosen with the whole group. Finish with these words:
- May we continue to find you, God, in all things, and may our music help us to know you more fully. We ask your blessing on all those who are gathered here and on all those who inspire us through their music.

9. Conclude by inviting the participants to join in singing the closing song.

Family connections

◆ Suggest that the participants invite their parents to listen to the song that they chose for this session and tell them why that particular song is important to them.

◆ Provide families with a blank CD or cassette tape, and some suggestions for creating a family soundtrack by recording favorite songs from each member of the family. They can then play the soundtrack on family trips or anytime the family will be together.

Mediaconnections

- Consider viewing the movie *Mr. Holland's Opus* (Hollywood Pictures, 143 minutes, 1996, rated PG), which tells the story of a teacher's passion for music and his commitment to passing it on to his students.
- The movie *Music of the Heart* (Miramax/Walt Disney Home Video, 124 minutes, 1999, rated PG) is a poignant film that helps to dispel the myth that young people do not enjoy classical music.

LIVE it!

Options and Actions

- **Broaden your horizons.** Check for community events featuring cultural, heritage, ethnic, or folk music. Provide the participants with a list, and encourage them to attend the event individually or as a group to learn more about a particular musical style.
- **Share your talent.** Host a talent show, an open band jam, or a karaoke night at your church.

Considering Your Music

Don't judge a person by their Walkman. When we judge or exclude others based on the music they listen to, we are not living by our Christian value of hospitality. God made all of us different, and we should celebrate those differences in one another and in the diversity of music that fills the world.

I can't believe it says that! We like the music, but what do we think about the words? One way to listen to music is to listen to the values in the words that we hear. Do we agree with those values? Are those the values of our family? our Church?

They're playing my song. Sometimes a song names our experience. This can happen when we feel good or when we feel bad. We can feel understood when someone else has a similar experience or feeling—that's true if the someone else is a friend or a music artist. When a song captures our own experience, it can remind us to act on the experience or emotion by praying about it, finding a Scripture passage that matches the experience, talking to a friend, or journaling.

Beware of a "junk" music diet. Music that we listen to affects our mood. Some songs bring us up, and some bring us down. Some music isn't good for us—it reinforces negative feelings toward others and ourselves. We should be careful when choosing the music that we listen to; like choosing the food that we eat, choosing with care the music that we listen to helps keep us healthy and connects us to others.

AT A GLANCE

Study It

**Core Session:
All Are Welcome**
(50 minutes)

- Puzzle Stations (20 minutes)
- Discussion (30 minutes)

Pray It

- Hands and Feet of Christ (15 minutes)

Live It

- Inclusion report card
- Friendship experiment

7 All Are Welcome

Overview

Everyone has had the experience of being excluded from a joke, a party, or an entire social group. For young people, the experience of being excluded can be painful. Youth ministry programs should strive to ensure that all young people are welcome, but this can be difficult to communicate to teenagers who interact with one another in many different settings. This session helps the participants identify the emotions of being left out. Drawing on this experience, the participants can begin to recognize the need to include others and to be welcoming and open to everyone.

Outcomes

- The participants will experience what it means to be left out.
- The participants will learn to be inclusive of all people.

Background Reading

- Scriptural connections: Matt. 7:1–5 (judging others), Rom. 14:7–12 (We do not live for ourselves.), Rom. 15:1–7 (Please others, not yourself.)
- *Catholic Youth Bible* article connections: "Living in Your Tent, on Your Holy Hill" (Ps. 15), "Are You for Real?" (Matt. 20: 1–16), "Stretch Me, Lord" (Acts 11:1–18)

Core Session:
All Are Welcome (50 minutes)

Puzzle Stations (20 minutes)

Preparation
- Gather the following items:
  - ❑ resource 4, "Puzzle Hints," three copies for each of the three stations
  - ❑ handout 4, "Puzzle Instructions," one copy for each of the three leaders
  - ❑ ten pencils, pens, or markers
  - ❑ two wooden spoons (or pencils)
  - ❑ envelopes, three for each of the three stations
  - ❑ newsprint, tape, and a marker
- Prior to the session, select three leaders to become familiar with the three puzzles used in the activity. They should completely understand the activity and practice it with others, to ensure they will not divulge the answer inadvertently. Instructions for each of the three puzzles are on handout 4, "Puzzle Instructions."
- Before the session, set up three stations in such a way that participants can move from one space to the next without overhearing what is happening at another station. Use the following instructions to set up each station:
  - ❑ Station 1: Chairs are set up auditorium style (with chairs facing a front "stage" area). You will need enough chairs for a third of the total number of participants. The leader sits on the floor in the front with the ten pencils.
  - ❑ Station 2: Chairs are set up in a circle. The number of chairs should equal a third of the total number of participants. The leader holds the two wooden spoons.
  - ❑ Station 3: Chairs are set up auditorium style, facing a front area where the leader will be sitting. The number of chairs should equal a third of the total number of participants.
- Before the session, copy and cut apart resource 4, "Puzzle Hints," for each game, and place the hints in envelopes. You will need three instruction envelopes for each station (one for each round of play).

1. Divide the participants into three groups of equal size. Explain that they will be asked to solve three different puzzles; then give the following instructions:
- Although you will be in a group, each of you will be asked to solve each of the puzzles individually. Do not ask other participants to reveal an answer or give you a hint.
- It is possible that some of you might know the answer to the puzzle or might figure it out quickly. If this is true, you can and should answer the questions that are asked by the leader. However, do not reveal the answer to the puzzle to anyone else.
- Each group will have only a few minutes with each puzzle, so pay attention, and try to figure out the puzzle quickly.

Ask the participants if they have any questions.

2. Instruct each group to go to a different station. When everyone has arrived at their station, the puzzle leaders should choose one group member to receive the hint. This should be done by publicly handing the hint to a young person and saying something like, "This should help you." When the person with the hint has had a chance to read it, the leader should begin the puzzle.

As the facilitator, you will need to keep track of and call time after 4 or 5 minutes. If many people solve the puzzles quickly, consider giving them less time. If few people are solving the puzzles (10 percent or less), additional time can be given. When the puzzle is over, the leader at each puzzle station does not reveal the answer to the participants, and instructs those who have solved it not to reveal the answer either.

3. Each group then moves to the next station, and the puzzle leaders pass out their hint. Continue with the instructions in step 2. As facilitator, call time after 4 or 5 minutes. Each group then moves to their last station and repeats step 2 a final time.

4. When you have called time after the third round, gather the participants together in chairs to talk about the activity.

Discussion (30 minutes)

1. Ask the following questions, and have a recorder write the responses from the participants on a sheet of newsprint:
- How are you feeling about the activity?
- Name some emotions or feeling words that describe your experience with the activity.

It is likely that many will be frustrated with not being able to solve one or more of the puzzles. Keep the participants from knowing the answers to the puzzles until later in the process. Ask these follow-up questions:

- For those of you who received one of the hint envelopes, how did you feel during that puzzle?
- For those of you who solved one (or all) of the puzzles, how did you feel?
- How many of you did not solve the numbers game puzzle?
- How many of you did not solve the open or closed puzzle?
- How many of you did not solve the bookkeepers club puzzle?
- How would you feel if I told you that I was not going to give you the answers to the puzzles?

2. When the participants have answered the preceding questions, have each of the station leaders do their puzzle one more time, although this time they should be as obvious as possible so that people can figure out the answer. Try to get everyone to understand the puzzle, but before moving on to the next puzzle, have the leader say the answer to the puzzle out loud so that no one is left out.

3. Lead the participants in a large-group discussion using the following questions:
- We had some fun with these puzzles, and you had the chance to experience either being left out or being part of the "in" crowd—those who knew the answers to the puzzles.
- At what times have you felt left out?
- When have you been part of the in crowd?
- When you were part of the in crowd, did you ever notice others being left out? What did you think about that?

4. Tape a sheet of newsprint to a wall, and write the phrase "What We Can Do" on it. Then ask the participants to share their response to the following question:
- Because many people have had the experience of being left out, and you know how that feels, what can you do to make sure that other people do not feel left out?

If you are doing this with a leadership team or a group that meets regularly, ask the following question:
- How can we, as a group, make sure that no one who comes to our program or group will ever feel left out?
- Write the participants' answers on the newsprint and post it in the regular meeting area.

5. Close the session with the following comments:
- This puzzle activity helped us connect to times when we may have felt left out of an activity or a group.
- Even though the puzzle activity was fun, it does help us see how hurtful it can be to friends and peers when they are left out of activities or social groups.

- We recognize that it's okay—and good—to be part of a group, whether it is friends, youth group members, classmates, or teammates. We have the opportunity to invite others to participate with us, to be included in our activities and programs.
- God's message to us is that none of us are on our own. We need one another, and when we don't include others and set them apart from the crowd, we are not doing God's will.
- We can each reach out to people in ways that will let them know we value them as people and believe them to be worthwhile and important to the whole community.
- As a group, we need to be attentive to those who are new to us, so that our jokes and stories, shared experiences, and good friendships are reasons why others are drawn to us—not made to feel left out. We must always work to include others.

Hands and Feet of Christ (15 minutes)

Preparation
- Gather the following:
  ❑ a *Catholic Youth Bible* or other Bible
  ❑ paper and a pencil for each participant
- Invite a participant to proclaim 2 Cor. 13:5–7.
- Prepare music leaders to lead an opening song. Possible song selections can be found in *"Spirit & Song* Connections."
- Before the start of prayer, give each participant a sheet of paper and a pencil.
- Arrange a prayer space so that the participants will have something to write on—either by setting them at tables or by giving them a book or another hard surface to write on.

   1. Begin by getting the group's attention, and then inviting prayer to begin with the opening song.

   2. Invite the reader to come forward and proclaim the Scripture passage. Allow a few moments of quiet reflection to follow.

Spirit & Song connections

◆ "Strength for the Journey," by Michael John Poirier
◆ "Shine, Jesus, Shine," by Graham Kendrick
◆ "Prayer of St. Francis," by Sebastian Temple

3. Read the following reflection, which is adapted from the article "A Spiritual Checkup," located near 2 Corinthians, chapter 13, in *The Catholic Youth Bible*.

- How often do you take a break from your life to do a spiritual checkup on your relationship with God, other people, and yourself? In the reading we just heard, Paul suggests that the Corinthians give themselves a test—and this is good advice for us today.
- On the paper you have received, you will have the opportunity to reflect on a few questions in order to conduct your own spiritual checkup. Because this is an opportunity for us to *stop* and reflect, we will use the four letters of the word *stop* to remind us of some areas of our life on which we need to reflect.

4. After sharing the following comments and questions with the participants, allow 2 to 3 minutes for prayerful reflection.

- **S** stands for Spirit. Are you aware that the Holy Spirit is always present to you and can be called on to help you make the right decisions in your life?
- **T** stands for think. Do you honestly think about how your actions and behaviors affect you, others, and your relationship with God?
- **O** stands for others. Do you make it a priority to reach out and support others, particularly those who are in greatest need?
- **P** stands for pray. Do you thank God for your blessings and for the struggles that make you stronger?

5. Conclude by asking the participants to bow their heads, and then share with them the following closing prayer.

- Saint Teresa of Ávila told us that we must be Jesus' hands, feet, and mouthpiece to the world. If we are to be for other people what God calls us to be, we must remember this saint's words. And so let us pray:

> Gracious and forgiving God, help us to be your hands and feet in the world. May others know of your Gospel by observing our lives. Make us strong enough to stand up for what is right, open enough to include everyone, and reflective enough to *stop* for a spiritual checkup from time to time. We ask you to forgive us for the times when we have not been welcoming of the stranger and the times when we have ignored someone in need of our friendship. Help us to become a friend to all. We ask this through your Son, our friend, Jesus Christ. Amen.

Familyconnections

Ask the participants to talk with their parents about what it was like to be left out when they were younger. Invite the families to talk about times and ways they have felt excluded in groups that they participate in—regardless of their age.

Mediaconnections

To look closely at the issue of cliques, stereotypes, and exclusion, the following movies could be viewed as a group, with a short discussion to follow:
- *Mask* (Universal Studios, 120 minutes, 1985, rated PG-13)
- *The Elephant Man* (Paramount Studio, 124 minutes, 1980, rated PG)
- *Ever After* (Fox Home Entertainment, 100 minutes, 1998, rated PG)
- *10 Things I Hate About You* (Touchstone Video, 97 minutes, 1999, rated PG-13)
- *She's All That* (Miramax Home Entertainment, 95 minutes, 1999, rated PG-13)

Options and Actions

- **Inclusion report card.** At a future meeting, in which many of the same participants who are present at this session are in attendance, pull out the newsprint sheet that was created, titled "What We Can Do." Ask the young people to give themselves a grade, either individually or as a group, that reflects how well they are doing the actions that they thought would be important for including others.
- **Friendship experiment.** Encourage the young people to befriend one of their peers whom they know is often excluded from social groups or activities at school, on a team, or in their neighborhood. Check in with the young person to find out how the experiment is going.

Puzzle Hints

Station 1: Numbers Game

This is a hint to help you solve the puzzle.

Ignore the pencils, and pay attention to the leader's hands.

Do not share this information with anyone.

Station 2: Open or Closed

This is a hint to help you solve the puzzle.

Ignore the spoons, and pay attention to the participants' legs.

Do not share this information with anyone.

Station 3: The Bookkeepers Club

This is a hint to help you solve the puzzle.

Pay attention to the letters within the words that are used. The name of this game is an additional hint.

Do not share this information with anyone.

Resource 4: Permission to reproduce for program use is granted. © 2004 by Saint Mary's Press.

Puzzle Instructions

Station 1: Numbers Game

You will need ten pencils.

Your goal is to confuse the participants into thinking that you are creating numbers through the use of the pencils when, in fact, the numbers will be revealed by your fingers.

Take the pencils (some or all) and arrange them in a design on the floor. Then in a subtle way, place your hands on the floor, extending some of your fingers on one or both hands. Ask the participants, "What number is this?" The correct answer is equal to the number of fingers that you have extended. If no one guesses the correct number within a few seconds, share the correct answer. Then rearrange the pencils, extend some of your fingers again, and ask, "What number is this?" Always tell them the correct answer so that people can begin to solve the puzzle. When the person who has the hint, or anyone else in the crowd, begins to figure out the puzzle, allow them to answer the question, and affirm them for the right answer.

A couple of things to keep in mind:
- You can arrange the pencils in any way that you want, and you do not need to create the same arrangement for the same number of extended fingers.
- One of the ways to confuse people is to create a design, extend, for example, three fingers, and ask, "What number is this?" Then rearrange the pencils, extend three different fingers, and ask, "What number is this?" Since three is the right answer for both, it will confuse people more.
- You can change the number of pencils that you use for different "numbers."
- Practice extending different fingers before doing the activity so that you do not use the same numbers all the time. Think about which fingers you are going to extend before placing your hands on the floor.
- You can also place your hands (with extended fingers) on your knees, if you want.

Station 2: Open or Closed

You will need two wooden spoons.

The goal of this game is to confuse the participants into thinking that the wooden spoons are the focus of this activity when, in fact, the legs of the participants will reveal the correct answers.

This activity is hard to describe but very easy to lead!

The activity is going to involve all the participants. The spoons will either be passed "open" or "closed." You will begin the activity by crossing or not crossing the spoons while handing them to the person on your left.

The participants will assume that the spoons will determine whether they are open or closed, when, in fact, it will depend on whether the person's legs are crossed or not crossed. For instance, you will pass the spoons to the person on your left and say, "I am passing these to you closed" (because their legs are crossed). The spoons can either be crossed or not—it does not matter, but focus your attention on the spoons. You then say to the person on your left, "Are you receiving them closed or open?" The person has to guess "open" or "closed." The correct answer will be "open" if their legs are not crossed, or "closed" if their legs are crossed. If the person answers correctly, say, "Yes." If the answer is incorrect, say, "No, you are receiving them (either open or closed)." Then ask, "And how will you pass the spoons?" The person will have to answer "open" or "closed." The correct answer to "How will you pass the spoons?" is related to the legs of the person to whom the spoons are being passed. If they are correct, say, "Yes." If their answer is incorrect, tell them, "No, you are passing them (either open or closed)."

Some things to expect and keep in mind:
- People will not understand how the spoons, which are passed from one person to another without changing form (they are passed crossed and the person receives them crossed), can change from closed to open.
- Encourage people to change the form of the spoons as they pass them, if they seem to just be passing them from one to another without doing anything with them.
- When it is your turn, cross or uncross your legs between receiving them and passing them. Others who have figured out the activity will copy your lead.
- Be careful not to really look at the legs of the people in the group. You want to keep the attention on the spoons.
- As people begin to understand the puzzle, let them help you answer yes or no to the other participants.
- If someone's legs are wide open, or if they are tightly crossed, you can use phrases like, "They are very open," or "They are very closed."

Station 3: The Bookkeepers Club

There are no supplies needed for this activity.

The goal of this activity is to have the participants try to figure out whether bookkeepers like certain items. The items that bookkeepers like always have two of the same letters next to each other. For instance, bookkeepers like kittens, books, and walls.

The leader begins the game by explaining that to belong to the Bookkeepers Club, they must know what they like and what they don't like.

The leader then uses examples to tell people what bookkeepers like and don't like.
- Bookkeepers like kittens but not cats.
- They like glasses but not cups.
- They like grass but not lawns.
- They like apples but not oranges.

After giving a few examples, the leader asks if others would like to take a guess. If they answer correctly, make a fuss about them being in the Bookkeepers Club. If they are incorrect, tell them they are wrong, and comment on their answers. For example:
- If the person says, "They like Jim but not Jerry," respond by telling him or her that bookkeepers like Jerry but are not fond of Jim.
- If the person says, "They like biographies but not fiction," respond by telling her or him that bookkeepers don't like either of those, but they do like books.
- If the person says, "They like walls but not floors," respond by telling him or her that bookkeepers like both.

Continue to give examples, and let others give examples.

Trust

Overview

Trust is the cornerstone of true community: when people trust each other, the bonds between them grow and true community is created. When trust fails to develop, or when trust is betrayed, the community experiences potentially devastating effects. Creating a climate of trust is one of the most important tasks of any community. This session is designed for groups that know one another but may not currently be sharing at a deep level. The participants will be encouraged to think about the ways in which trust enhances relationships. They will be involved in an activity to help them know one another better, and they will be encouraged to share at a deeper level. The session works best with a group whose members have already expressed a desire to know one another better, and where some small measure of trust already exists.

Outcomes

- The participants will have the opportunity to share information about themselves.
- The participants will explore the role of trust in relationships.
- The participants will have the opportunity to reflect on their own trustworthiness.

Background Reading

- Scriptural connections: Ps. 62 (Trust in God alone.), Isa. 43:1–5 (protection from God)
- *Catholic Youth Bible* article connections: "Ultimate Trust in God!" (Gen. 22:1–19), "Believing" (Ps. 14), "Consistent and Trustworthy" (Gal. 2:11–14)

AT A GLANCE

Study It

Core Session: Building Trust (55 minutes)
- Trust in Society (20 minutes)
- Trust Activity (20 minutes)
- Being Trustworthy (15 minutes)

Session Extensions
- Trust Fall (20 minutes)
- Trust Maze (20 minutes)

Pray It

- Walking with Jesus (10 minutes)

Core Session: Building Trust (55 minutes)

Preparation
- Gather the following items:
  - ❑ newsprint and markers, enough for each group of four to have one sheet and a marker, and additional newsprint for other activities
  - ❑ masking tape
- Create a newsprint sheet that lists the information from resource 5, "Elements of Trust."

Trust in Society (20 minutes)

1. Welcome the participants and gather them into a large group. Introduce the session in this way:
- Today we are going to look at the role of trust in relationships. Trust is an essential part of any community. Trust is the backbone of a community's relationship with its members.
- If trust does not exist, we find an overwhelming climate of suspicion, in which people are guarded with each other. Trust is something that develops over time. Real community is only possible when trust exists between people.
- To live in the world today, we have to trust a lot of different people. They may share values and beliefs different from our own, yet we still need to learn to trust others.
- It would be impossible to carry on our daily life without trusting others. Perhaps without realizing it, we put our trust in many different people each and every day.

2. Divide the participants into groups of four. Give each group a sheet of newsprint and a marker. Have each group brainstorm a list of all the people they have contact with (either personally or as a member of a community) and in whom they put their trust. Some examples would be other drivers, airplane pilots, news broadcasters, teachers, game officials, police officers, firefighters, church leaders, parents and siblings, and friends. Allow about 5 minutes for the groups to work.

Try This

If your group is larger than thirty people, it will be difficult to do this session. Subdivide the group into two or more smaller groups, and then conduct the session. Bring the groups together at the end to share their list of needed actions for trustworthiness. Make the closing comments with the whole group, and have everyone pray together.

3. When the groups have completed their work, invite everyone back to a common area. Have each group present their list to the other participants. Afterward hang each sheet of newsprint on a nearby wall.

4. When all the lists have been presented, ask the participants these questions:
- Why do we trust these people?
- Are there any people listed on another group's list that you do not trust? Why?
- Why is it important, as a society, that we trust others? What would happen if we did not trust others?
- Is it harder or easier to trust people you do not know?

5. Using the participants responses to the preceding questions as a guide, conclude this activity with the following comments:
- Trust is an essential part of any community. Without trusting others we could not easily move through our days and our world.
- We often trust people without knowing them personally. We put our trust in a title or a job, based on the good work that others in that job have done in the past. For instance, we trust firefighters because we have seen proof that they are trustworthy (the terrorist attack of September 11, 2001, for example).
- In this community we must constantly work on building the trust we share. We do this by taking risks with what we share and being trustworthy with information that is shared by others. Some important elements can build trust within a group, and some specific things can decrease the levels of trust.

Trust Activity (20 minutes)

1. To begin the activity, ask everyone to find a partner and stand with him or her. (It is easiest if you have an even number of participants for this activity, so you might want to have an extra adult who can participate if necessary.) When all the participants have found a partner, introduce the activity in this way:
- When we begin, you will be asked to join hands with your partner. You must keep your hands joined whenever you are with a partner, unless you are doing an activity. When you are with your partner, you may hear one of the following commands. (Note: It will be helpful to have one pair demonstrate these directions.)
  - *Face-to-face.* When you hear this, stand face-to-face with your partner with your hands joined.

- *Back-to-back.* When you hear this, turn your bodies so that you are back-to-back with your partner. Keep your hands joined when you are moving from the face-to-face stance to the back-to-back stance.
- *Switch partners.* When you hear this, quickly find a new partner, and stand in the same position with your new partner as you left your previous partner. This means that if you were back-to-back with your previous partner, then you should stand back-to-back with your hands joined with your new partner.
- *Activity.* When you hear this, you will be given directions for the trust activity that you are invited to do with your partner. It is important to remember that trust gets built because of thousands of little things that happen between people. This activity will invite you to engage in all sorts of little "risks" with members of this group. When an activity is suggested, if you are willing to do it, simply go ahead and do the activity. If you are not willing to do the activity, simply say to your partner, "Pass," but stay with that person until the next command is given. You are free to pass at any time, but you are also encouraged to take a few risks during the activity.
- Make sure the participants understand what you are asking them to do by giving them time to ask questions.

2. Invite the participants to join hands with their partners. To start the activity, make it fun and active by having them move from face-to-face and back-to-back a few times with their original partner before calling "switch partners." Continue in this manner until they get to their third partner before calling out an activity. The following activities should be added to the other three commands so that as participants move between partners, sometimes they will have an activity and sometimes they will not. Each of these activities should take only a short amount of time, so it is important to keep the activity moving. The activities are as follows, and should be called out in this order:

- Look deeply into your partner's eyes, and don't stop for 20 seconds.
- Lean on your partner while balancing on one foot.
- Tell your partner a dream that you have for your future.
- Make the sign of the cross on your partner's forehead, and say, "God bless you."
- Tell your partner something good about yourself.
- Give your partner a big hug.
- Reveal to your partner something at which you are really bad.
- The shorter person in the pair does a trust fall. Keeping your feet together and your arms folded across your chest, fall backward into the arms of your partner. (Remind the participants to be extra careful with this activity, as carelessness could cause injury).

- The taller person in the pair lies on the floor. The shorter person jumps over the taller partner three times. (Remind the participants to be extra careful with this activity, as carelessness could cause injury).
- Tell your partner about a time when you were really sad or hurt. (Give more time for this question.)
- Tell your partner about your relationship with God. (Give more time for this question.)

3. When all the activities are finished, keep the young people with their current partner and ask them to take a seat (preferably on the floor). If possible, arrange the participants in a circle, or at least a semicircle so they can see one another better. Explain that you want to ask them some questions, and if their answer to the question is yes, they should raise their hand; if their answer is no, they should keep their hand lowered. No one should talk during this time. Ask the following questions:

- Did you pass on any of the activities?
- Were you uncomfortable during any of the activities?
- Did you find the activities in which you had to touch your partner difficult?
- Did you find sharing personal information with your partner difficult?
- Did you find the activities difficult when your physical safety was dependent on another?
- Did it get easier to do the activities as time went on?

When you have completed the questions, ask the participants if they would like to comment on any of their answers. If they have no comments, you might want to follow up with the following questions, to be answered verbally.

- What does all of this say about trust?
- Why is it difficult to trust others?
- Why is it easy to trust others?

4. End with the following comments (if they were not previously mentioned by the participants):

- Creating community among people means that we have to trust others in many different ways—with our physical safety; with our ideas, fears, and dreams; and by sharing our personal space with them. People will have different comfort levels with each of these areas of trust for many different reasons, but we can all expand that comfort level as we grow in our relationship with others.
- The more we know others, the easier it becomes to trust them. Trust also gets easier when we find we are in a trustworthy group. If others show us that we are valued and safe in their presence, it is easy to trust them.

- Trust is built among people in lots of easy ways; and in lots of equally easy ways, trust gets broken among people. Our next activity will help us look at our own trustworthiness.

Being Trustworthy (15 minutes)

1. Begin this activity by asking the participants to return to their partner from the previous activity. (They should already be sitting next to the person.) Remind the participants that they are trying to build trust with each other, and therefore the question they are being asked will demand that they be willing to trust each other. Ask them to share with each other a time when they were untrustworthy. Some examples might be sharing information with another that was supposed to be kept secret, lying to someone (through words or through omission), or cheating on schoolwork or during an athletic event. Give each pair about 5 minutes to share.

2. In a large group, engage the participants in talking about the consequences of their untrustworthiness, for example, perhaps they have lost a friend or people have refused to share important information with them. Post their answers on newsprint. People should not necessarily tell about their situation in answering the following questions:
- What were the consequences of your untrustworthiness to you personally?
- What were some of the consequences to the others involved?
- Were there any long-term effects?

3. Ask the participants to create a list of things they have learned about why it is important to be trustworthy. Ask the following question, posting the answers on newsprint:
- What do I have to do to be worthy of another's trust?

4. Close the activity by posting the newsprint sheet that you created from resource 5, "Elements of Trust," next to the list that the young people have created. Invite them to compare the two lists and note similarities and differences. Ask them to think about one thing on either list that they would like to improve. Ask them to hold on to that thought as they move into prayer. Then make the following comments:
- As a group, we hope the trust that exists among us will continue to grow. If that is to happen, we all have to prove ourselves worthy of each other's trust. Building this trust is an important task that lies ahead for each of us.
- We also take a risk in sharing information about ourselves and in trusting our safety to those around us. If we all work hard at being trustworthy, taking those risks will become easier.
- We can learn much about trust from God. Let us move to prayer to connect with God and to end our session.

Session Extensions

Trust Fall (20 minutes)

   1. Ask the participants to participate in a trust fall. Before beginning, remind them that this activity can be dangerous and that everyone needs to take it seriously. Provide them with the following instructions:
- Please get into groups of about eight people. Designate a "faller."
- If you are the faller, stand with your feet together and your arms across your chest. Close your eyes.
- Each member of the group needs to stand in a tight circle around the faller, creating a distance of about 2 feet between the circle and the faller. Put your arms out in front of you, with your palms up (to create a flat surface for the faller).
- When I say, "Fall," the fallers should keep their back straight and fall in any direction. The group's job is to catch the faller, and then gently move that person in a different direction. The faller will be gently passed from one side of the circle to another.
- During the activity you may replace the faller with other members of the circle.

   2. In a large group, talk about the trust-fall activity with the participants by asking the following questions:
- What happened during this activity?
- Was it hard to trust? Why or why not?
- What is demanded of you in order to trust?
- What made it possible for you to trust others?
- How did you know you could trust the others?

   3. Close with the following comments:
- Trust makes it possible to do things with people that we would not ordinarily do. That might mean falling into their arms, but it also might mean sharing with them something important about ourselves or confiding a dream or simply feeling calm and relaxed in their presence.
- When we really trust another, amazing things are possible.

Trust Maze (20 minutes)

Preparation
- Gather the following items:
  - ❑ one blindfold
  - ❑ jacks, about fifty
- Create a maze with the jacks so you have a curved path through the jacks. The maze should allow the person to walk about 10 feet, and should be

created in a space where the participants cannot see it prior to participating in the activity.

1. Ask for a volunteer. Ask the volunteer to remove her or his shoes. Blindfold the individual. Remind the participants that the volunteer could get hurt and that everyone must be careful. Move the entire group (including the volunteer) into the space where the maze is located. Tell the volunteer that you have created a maze out of jacks, and that she or he will have to depend on the group's directional commands to move from the start of the maze to the end. Explain to the group that it is their job to move the volunteer through the maze without having the person step on a jack (which would hurt a lot). Clarify any questions. When everyone is ready, you can begin. When the task has been completed, you can blindfold another person, rearrange the maze, and repeat the activity.

2. Give several young people the opportunity to participate, and then process the trust-maze activity by discussing the following questions with the participants in a large group:
- What happened during this activity?
- (To the volunteers): Was it hard for you to trust the group?
- What was demanded of you in order to trust?
- What made it possible to trust others?
- Is it harder to trust a whole group than it would be to trust an individual?

3. Make the following comments:
- Trust makes it possible to do things with people that ordinarily we would not do. That might mean walking through danger while others lead the way, but it also might mean sharing with them something important about yourself, confiding a hope or a dream, or simply feeling calm and relaxed in their presence.
- When we really trust others, amazing things are possible. Think about teams that win championships or climb mountains—none of that would be possible without trust.

Pray It

Walking with Jesus (10 minutes)

Preparation
- Gather the following item:
  ❑ a *Catholic Youth Bible* or other Bible

Spirit & Song connections

- "Amazing Grace," by John Newton
- "Be Not Afraid," by Bob Dufford, SJ
- "Lord of All Hopefulness," by Timothy R. Smith

- Invite a participant to proclaim Matt. 14:22–33.
- Ask for a volunteer to be the prayer leader.
- Invite a participant to read the petitions.

1. Get the group's attention, and then invite prayer to begin with a silent sign of the cross.

2. Invite the reader to come forward and proclaim the Scripture reading. Allow a few moments of silence to follow.

3. Then invite the prayer leader to share the following reflection:
- If you know the disciple Peter, it is not surprising that he was willing to take the risk of stepping out of the boat to Jesus. But why does Peter start to sink? When he is focused on Jesus, everything is fine. It is when he takes his eyes off Jesus, and notices the fierce wind, that Peter begins to sink.
- Jesus invites you to risk a relationship with him. You have to step out in faith. Perhaps you need to move in the direction of being more worthy of others' trust by leaving some old ways behind.
- Learn from Peter to keep your focus on Jesus. As the disciples learned, this is no ordinary man; this is the Son of God!
- Following Jesus might get scary or difficult at times, but all great adventures involve some risk, and there is no greater adventure than being a disciple.

(Adapted from "Do You Trust Jesus?" near Matt. 14:22–33, in *The Catholic Youth Bible*)

4. Invite the reader of the petitions to come forward. Tell the participants that they should respond to each petition by saying, "Lord, give us courage." The petitions are as follows:
- Give us, Lord, the courage we need to trust the others in this group more deeply so we can grow together in community. We pray . . .
- Give us, Lord, the courage we need to change the things we do in our lives that destroy the trust people have in us. We pray . . .
- Give us, Lord, the courage to look at strangers with eyes of trust, seeing through those things that make us different to find the things that bind us together. We pray . . .
- Give us, Lord, the courage to share ourselves, all that is good and holy about us, with those of this community and with all those we meet, so they can see the goodness you have planted within us. We pray . . .
- Give us, Lord, the courage to get out of the boat and follow your Son, to live lives that are generous and loving and kind. We pray . . .

5. Close by holding hands and praying the Our Father together.

Media connections

To look closely at the role trust plays in relationships, the following movies could be viewed, with a short group discussion to follow:

- *As Good as It Gets* (Columbia/Tristar Studios, 139 minutes, 1997, rated PG-13). The main characters in this movie become friends and learn what it means to rely on someone else.
- *K19: The Widowmaker* (Paramount Home Video, 138 minutes, 2002, rated PG-13). In this movie two people learn to trust each other aboard a Soviet nuclear submarine.
- *Harry Potter and the Sorcerer's Stone* (Warner Home Video, 152 minutes, 2001, rated PG). Three young students become friends in this movie, and learn to count on one another.

Elements of Trust

Elements that help build trust:
- Being willing to share personal information about yourself.
- Being respectful of information that others share with you.
- Holding information you hear from others in confidence.
- Being consistent in your behavior toward others.
- Doing what you say you are going to do (following through on commitments).
- Affirming and accepting others for who they are.
- Being trustworthy and honest.

Elements that prevent or break down trust:
- Rejecting or ridiculing other people or their ideas.
- Disrespecting others through your actions or words.
- Judging others because of their abilities or ideas.
- Stereotyping people based on clothing, personal preferences, color of skin, and so on.

9 Catholic and American

Overview

In this session the participants look at the responsibilities of being Catholic and American, and how the Church challenges us to participate in our local community to make it a better place to live. The participants look at the rights of all human beings, and discuss ways they can get involved in their community, now and in the future, to protect and advocate for these rights.

Outcomes

- The participants will reflect on the importance of participating in their own community for the common good.
- The participants will understand the moral responsibility we have as Catholics to participate in civic life, and will begin to articulate issues that are important to all citizens.
- The participants will learn ways they can actively participate in the community now and in the future.

Background Reading

- Scriptural connections: Matt. 25:31–46 (You did it to me.), Luke 1:46–55 (Mary's Magnificat)
- *Catholic Youth Bible* article connections: "Saving Lives" (Exod. 1:15–22), "Jesus and Civil Disobedience" (Matt. 21:12–13)

AT A GLANCE

Study It

Core Session: Catholic and American (50 minutes)

- A Perfect World (20 minutes)
- Rights and Responsibilities (20 minutes)
- Get Involved (10 minutes)

Pray It

- Taking It to the Streets (10 minutes)

Live It

- Get the vote out
- Speak up and speak out
- Tomorrow's headlines

Core Session: Catholic and American (50 minutes)

Preparation
- Gather the following items:
  - ❏ copies of handout 5, "Our Human Rights: The Basics," one for each participant
  - ❏ paper and markers for each small group of seven participants
  - ❏ a CD player and a CD with reflective instrumental music
- List the following items on a sheet of newsprint or a chalkboard:
  - ❏ Look for information in newspapers, magazines, and reference materials to learn about the issues.
  - ❏ Participate in a political discussion.
  - ❏ Write letters to elected representatives.
  - ❏ Attend meetings to gain information, discuss issues, or lend support.
  - ❏ Campaign for a candidate.
  - ❏ Register to vote when you are eighteen, and vote for candidates that share your values.
  - ❏ Register for the draft when you are eighteen.
  - ❏ Help organize a "register to vote" campaign at your high school or community center.
  - ❏ Demonstrate for issues you support and believe in through marches, boycotts, sit-ins, or other forms of nonviolent protest.
  - ❏ Join a group that advocates for a specific issue (Amnesty International, a local Right to Life chapter, a human concerns committee).

A Perfect World (20 minutes)

1. Divide the participants into groups of seven. Tell the participants that their small groups' task is to come up with a vision for the perfect world. This vision should include ideas from everyone in the group, and it should reflect the values that the group shares, including religious values and family values. Tell the participants that they will have about 10 minutes to work on their vision. Make sure you do not give any more details about the contents of the session.

2. After 2 minutes of group work, quietly remove two members from each group by tapping them on the shoulder and asking them to leave the group. They should stay in the room, but they are no longer allowed to participate in the group activity. They should be instructed to sit quietly and observe. Give them no explanation as to why they are not allowed to participate. After another 2 to 3 minutes, remove another pair from each group in the same manner, with no explanation as to why they can no longer participate. Repeat this process until only one person remains in each group. It is best to accomplish this in three rounds. Make sure to encourage those who are in a group to keep to the task, even though they may have questions about why people are being removed. If nonparticipants have questions, ignore them.

3. When only one participant remains, have that person finish up the vision. Invite the people who are left in the small groups to share their group's vision of the perfect world with the large group. Be sure to introduce it as the whole group's vision. This should incite grumbling from the "nonparticipants," especially those who were removed at the beginning of the exercise.

4. When each group has shared their "perfect world," gather everyone into one group and ask the following questions:
- What was it like for those of you who were asked to stop participating? How did it feel to have no input?
- Did the vision that your group came up with include your values?
- How did your group change when people started leaving?
- Was it easier or harder to include other people's ideas when they were not in the group anymore?

5. Close this activity by pointing out that it is hard to be assured that your thoughts are reflected in a group project if you are not allowed to participate. The same is true for our society. If you are not allowed to participate, or if you choose not to, your voice will be missed and your ideas will be lost. Make the following comments to the participants:
- In this session we are going to take a look at our responsibility as Catholics to participate in our community. When people were removed from the groups in our activity, they no longer had a voice in the project. When we do not participate in our communities, we remove our voice from our community. In fact, the United States Catholic bishops, in their statement *Faithful Citizenship: Civic Responsibility for a New Millennium,* have written that we have a moral responsibility to participate in our communities and to make sure the values of the Gospel are heard in our world today.

- As Americans we are blessed with a government that provides lots of opportunities to get involved and also encourages us to do so. We can vote, we can involve ourselves in peaceful protests, we can attend and speak at meetings about community problems, and we can write letters to politicians, just to name a few. (You may also wish to have the participants name all the ways they can get involved.)

Rights and Responsibilities (20 minutes)

1. Invite the participants to return to their original small group. Distribute handout 5, "Our Human Rights: The Basics," to each person. Read through the handout with the participants, and explain that each one of the rights listed also has corresponding responsibilities.

2. Have each small group choose two or three rights, and then ask them to brainstorm what the responsibilities are for each of the rights. You might want to provide each group with a sheet of paper and a marker for recording purposes. Remind them to include individual responsibilities as well as community responsibilities. You may want to provide the following example:

- One of the rights is the right to act according to your conscience. Individually, we are responsible to inform our conscience and to listen to our conscience. In addition, communities must strive not to put people in situations where they are not allowed to act on their own conscience.

This is a simple example, but it illustrates the task. Give the small groups 15 minutes to complete this task.

3. Have each small group choose a spokesperson to come forward and share their work with the entire group. Make sure each spokesperson names the rights the small group chose and notes whether the responsibilities are individual or community responsibilities.

4. Make the following comments:
- The challenge of protecting rights and living up to our responsibilities is a difficult one, but one that we must accept to fully live out our Catholic faith.
- Our faith calls us to be a part of the larger world that we live in. We must worry not only about ourselves but also we must focus on those who are less fortunate, those without a voice in society, and all the people of the world.
- God made us interdependent. When we fail to participate in society, we are failing to live our call to community.
- It is important to recognize that the decisions we make as a society have a great effect on people and the opportunities they have to live a life that is respectful of their right to participate fully in decisions that will affect them.

Get Involved (10 minutes)

  1. Offer the following comments:
- Remember at the beginning of this session when we talked about how important it is to participate in our communities and bring our values to the world?
- After looking at some of our values, namely the rights of human beings, it is obvious that defending these rights is a big job. In fact, defending rights requires more than the work of just one or two people. That is why it is so important that all of us get involved.
- Take a few moments to reflect on the fundamental human rights listed on handout 5, and come up with an individual action plan of things you can do. Be sure to make a decision on what particular issues are important to you and what kinds of things you can do to use your gifts and talents.

You might consider playing some soft, reflective music in the background. Allow 3 to 5 minutes.

  2. Regather the group, and ask the participants to share their ideas. Then share the list that you prepared on newsprint or a chalkboard. If the young people mentioned some good ideas, you might want to add them to the sheet of newsprint.

  3. Close this activity by saying:
- Being a Catholic in the world can be a challenge because our faith requires that we go into the world and make it a better place.
- We have a moral responsibility to use our voice and our gifts in our communities.
- We see in the Scriptures that Jesus was active in his society (overturning the tables in the Temple, teaching in the Temple, interacting with the leaders of his day), trying to make the world he lived in a better place. We, similarly, are called to be active in our communities.
- If we carry out our action plans, we will be making a difference immediately. We don't have to wait until we are older to make a difference.

  4. Invite the group to join in prayer:
- Let us now move to prayer to ask God for the strength and the courage to carry out our action plans.

Spirit & Song connections

- "What Is Our Service to Be," by Scot Crandal
- "Holy Is Your Name," arranged by David Haas

Pray It

Taking It to the Streets (10 minutes)

Preparation
- Gather the following items:
  - ❑ 3-inch-by-5-inch index cards and pens, one of each for each participant
  - ❑ a *Catholic Youth Bible* or other Bible
  - ❑ a small table and a tablecloth
  - ❑ a candle and matches
  - ❑ a CD player and a CD of quiet, reflective music
- Place the Bible on the table, perhaps on a stand, in a prominent place in the room.
- Invite one of the participants to proclaim the Scripture reading, Matt. 21:12–13.

   1. Invite the participants to gather in a circle around the Bible. Distribute to each a blank index card and a pen. Ask them to put those items aside for the time being. Allow a few minutes for everyone to settle down and recognize the presence of God in their midst. Quietly light the candle.

   2. Introduce the prayer with these or similar comments:
- Sometimes when we think of Jesus, we do not think of him getting involved in his community and pushing for change. Yet the Gospels are filled with story of Jesus "pushing the envelope" and calling others to radical transformation. Let's listen to a short story in Matthew's Gospel, in which Jesus does just that.

   3. Invite the preselected young person to come forward and proclaim the Scripture reading. Allow a few moments of silence to follow.

   4. Offer the following reflection on the reading:
- When Jesus cleansed the Temple, he was stepping into the center of the community and making a stand. He performed an action that changed what was going on there.
- Although we may not be called to overturn tables, we are called to change our communities for the better.

- I invite each of you to take some quiet, reflective time and write one word on your index card that captures what you need from God in order to bring your voice to the community (for example, courage, or more information on a particular topic).

5. When all the participants have written on their cards, invite them to fold the card in half and, one at a time, come forward and lay it next to the Bible as a sign of their commitment to fuller community involvement. You may wish to play some quiet, reflective music while this ritual is taking place.

6. When everyone has finished, invite the participants to stand in a circle and pray the Lord's Prayer together. Conclude the prayer with a sign of peace.

Options and Actions

- **Get the vote out.** Organize a campaign in your local community—in cooperation with high schools, other churches, and community centers—to register people (especially young adults) to vote.
- **Speak up and speak out.** Organize an advocacy campaign about a local, national, or global issue. Study the issue through speakers or on-site visits, creating public service announcements or other types of publicity, writing letters to elected officials, attending community meetings, and talking with local government representatives.
- **Tomorrow's headlines.** Invite the participants to write headlines for tomorrow's newspaper announcing a country where the rights and needs of all citizens are met. Display those headlines in a prominent location in the church or parish center.

Familyconnections

♦ Suggest that families look through a week's worth of newspapers and identify places in their community where the rights of others are nonexistent or being abused. Suggest that families create a list of small action steps they can take to address these situations.

♦ Provide families with the materials to make a family scrapbook showing how each family invests their time, energy, and talents in the community. Gather the pages each family has created to make a parish family scrapbook.

Mediaconnections

Check out the following Web sites that promote community involvement: *www.rockthevote.org* and *www.project.org*. You might also encourage the participants to conduct an Internet search, and create a list of additional organizations and agencies that promote citizen involvement.

Our Human Rights: The Basics

All human beings, because they are created in the image and likeness of God, are created with a dignity that can never be taken away. It is a dignity we must help to protect. This dignity means that all human beings have a right to certain things. They have a right to:
- life
- food
- clothing
- decent and affordable housing
- have a family and the ability to take care of it
- a good education
- work (and to be paid enough to live decently)
- respect
- a good reputation
- privacy
- act according to their conscience
- freedom, including freedom of religion

(Adapted from the Vatican Council II document *Pastoral Constitution on the Church in the Modern World [Gaudium et Spes]*, 1965, number 26, at *www.vatican.va/archive/hist_councils/ ii_vatican_council/documents/vat-ii_cons_19651207_gaudium-et-spes_en.html*, accessed May 27, 2003)

10 The Changing Face of Friendship

Overview

This session is intended for juniors and seniors in high school, to help them deal with the changes in friendships that may occur as they leave high school and move into college, the military, or a job setting. The session invites the participants to celebrate their current friendships, prepares them for changes that may happen in the days to come, and provides them with a chance to think about what kind of relationship opportunities will be available to them in the future. This session works best when it involves friends in talking and thinking about the future. Consider using this session with parish youth-ministry leadership teams, retreat teams, graduating seniors, or any other group that has spent significant time together.

Outcomes

- The participants will identify the traits they most cherish in their friends.
- The participants will prayerfully celebrate their friends.
- The participants will plan for the future by considering the opportunities that are available to them.

Background Reading

- Scriptural connections: Ps. 23 (Surely goodness and mercy follow me.), 1 Cor. 1:4–9 (I give thanks to God for you.), Phil. 1:3–11 (I thank God every time I remember you.)
- *Catholic Youth Bible* article connections: "Jesus Is with Us!" (Luke 24: 13–35), "A Prayer for Friends" (John, chap. 17), "Send Us Your Spirit" (Acts 1:1–11)

AT A GLANCE

Study It

Core Session: The Changing Face of Friendship (50 minutes)
- Memory Lane (15 minutes)
- The Ties That Bind (20 minutes)
- Old and New (15 minutes)

Pray It

- A Time for Every Season Under Heaven (20 minutes)

Live It

- Celebrate friends
- Honor experiences

Core Session: The Changing Face of Friendship (50 minutes)

Preparation
- Gather the following items:
  - ❏ paper, one sheet for each participant
  - ❏ crayons or markers, at least one for each participant
  - ❏ newsprint (for large-group and small-group work)
  - ❏ markers
- If desired, invite a young adult to prepare a short witness talk to end the "Ties That Bind" activity. He or she should reflect on the questions the young people will be answering throughout this session as well as the comments that are listed at the end of the activity. You will need to be aware that including the witness talk will extend the time for this activity.

Memory Lane (15 minutes)

1. Gather the participants into a large group. Introduce the session with these or similar comments:

- Look around the room. Notice all the people who have gathered here. Think about the first time you met some of these people. What were your first impressions?

Allow time for the participants to respond.

- Much has changed since we first met, and we have shared a great deal during our time together. We are not the same people we were when we first met, and our relationships with one another have grown.
- We have gathered today because we all recognize that change is in the air. It will not be long before things change in our lives and friendships.

It would be appropriate to name some of those changes, including seniors who are graduating, the end of the youth ministry core team year, and friends who will be moving away.

- Today you will have some time to think about the treasures you have found in your friends and to celebrate those people in your life.
- We will also take a few moments to think about what the future holds, in terms of both continuing the friendships you currently have and making new friends in the future.

2. Give all the participants a sheet of paper and some crayons or markers. Then provide the following directions:
- We are going to spend a little time going down memory lane. To do this well, and to give you time to think and remember, I am going to ask you to do this activity in silence. We will talk about it afterward.
- I am going to ask you to think about people and situations, and then I will invite you to answer my questions in pictures, designs, images, or words. You are free to be as creative as possible, but if you are not very artistic, feel free to simply write names and words on the paper. There is no particular order to this activity, so you are free to use the paper however you wish. Any questions?
- To begin, please close your eyes for a moment and think about the friend that you feel closest to at this moment. (Pause for 20 seconds.) Now open your eyes and draw or write something about that person.

Give the participants a minute to draw. Continue with the following questions, allowing the participants about 20 seconds to think, and then time to draw or write about the experience or person:
- Thinking about the people you are closest to right now, how did you become friends with them? What activities, experiences, or interests did you have in common?
- If you have a whole group of friends you feel close to, what is it that binds you all together?
- How are you a better person today because of your friendships?
- Think about five people who are good friends to you. If you could say only one thing about each of those five, what is the thing you most value about each person?

3. Ask the participants to find a partner and spend 5 minutes sharing the words and pictures on their papers. Make sure that both participants have the opportunity to share.

The Ties That Bind (20 minutes)

1. Ask the participants to gather as a large group. Invite them to tell you what they think is the most important bond—a commonality that draws them together—with their friends. List those ideas on newsprint. Some ideas may include participation in sports teams, youth ministry groups, retreat teams, school classes, or shared experiences such as class trips, faith in God, the National Catholic Youth Conference (NCYC), or others.

2. Talk about the change that is coming (in other words, soon you will be graduating, your year as a leadership team will be ending, you will be going away to college, and so on). Ask the participants to look over the list and share those things that will be changing for them in the future. Ask them to cross out anything on the list that the participants will no longer have in common. (Note to facilitator: Cross out things like sports teams, youth ministry groups, school—these will automatically change. Do not cross out something like faith in God—even though it is *possible* that that could change.)

3. Make the following comments:
- We have crossed out all the things that will be changing in the near future. You will no longer have these things [name them] to link you together.
- Do you want to add anything to the list—things you did not think of initially—that will continue to bond you to your friends?

Add these ideas to the newsprint list.

4. At this point in the activity, the participants will have generated a list of things that connect people to one another that are not activities (in other words, faith in God, values, common interests, past experiences). Lead the young people in a discussion by asking the following questions:
- Why are the things on our newsprint so important?
- Are these things enough to maintain your friendships?
- What do you think will change in the future? Why?
- Will some friendships diminish or fade away in the years to come? Why?
- Will some friendships grow in the years to come? Why?

Using the information and conversation from these questions, sum up the discussion with the following closing thoughts, or have a young adult give a short witness talk about their own experience with the preceding questions, including the following comments:
- Some friendships do last a lifetime—but even those relationships ebb and flow. When our life circumstances change, we often change as well, and friendships will look and feel different because of that change. Do not worry—change is good!
- Just because some friends stop holding the same place in our lives, it does not mean they are no longer "real" friends. There will be people whom we will always remember with fondness, even if we see them only occasionally or never see them again. The bonds created between good friends always leave us feeling connected to each other. Perhaps you have experienced this already with friends who have moved away or classmates from grade school whom you do not see often.
- As we move into the future, we will need to be open to the gifts new people can and will bring into our lives. The people who are so important to us now were once strangers to us. There is no reason to let go of people, but do not close yourself off to new friends who will be entering your life in the future.

- One of the most important things that bind you together with your friends is your common faith in God and common values. To quote Michael W. Smith's song, "Friends are friends forever, if the Lord is the Lord of them" (*The First Decade: 1983–1993,* Meadowgreen Music Company [ASCAP]). The bonds of friendship are made stronger because we have seen the face of God in them.
- We can do things to keep our friendships strong—even amid the changes we will be experiencing.

Depending on the conversation preceding these comments, specifically around the "What do you think will change?" question, it might be appropriate to add these comments:

- One of the biggest changes as you go to college, into the military, or into the job market may be that the support you feel in your faith life can fall away. Without the regular contact you have with your parish through youth ministry programs, it can be easy to feel disconnected. This is even truer if you are going away from home and will have to establish yourself within a new parish community.
- You will meet many new people in the future, and all will not share your faith or the level of commitment you feel to being Catholic. When this happens, it is easy to feel isolated or to wish for what used to be.
- You can take responsibility for your faith life by connecting with a church or a Newman Center at your school or in the military, and you can continue to find ways to connect to your parish community throughout the year (if you are at home) or during breaks and vacations.
- You can also look to each other to provide support on the faith journey. You are lucky to know other people your own age who value the Catholic faith and who are willing to struggle through faith questions with you. Rely on each other in the years ahead to walk this journey of faith. You will inevitably find yourself asking new questions, struggling with moral issues, and looking for ways to grow in faith. Being able to share your faith journey with good friends will be important.

Old and New (15 minutes)

1. Divide the participants into small groups of six. Give each group a sheet of newsprint and a marker. Ask one person in each group to serve as the recorder and to divide the sheet of newsprint into two columns. Have the recorder title the left column, "Keep the Old," and then say:
- Brainstorm the things you will do in the future to maintain the friendships you now have. Be as creative as you wish—including individual ideas and group ideas.

Allow 3 minutes for the groups to complete this task.

2. Have the recorder title the second column, "Welcome the New," and then say:
- Brainstorm ideas of what you will do in the future to make new friends. In other words, what values will you look for in new friends, what activities will you join, how will you be open to new people?

Allow 3 minutes for the groups to complete this task.

3. If you have only a few small groups, ask each group to report everything that is on their lists. If you have more than four groups, ask each group to pick their top three ideas from both lists. Invite the groups to report on the "Keep the Old" column first, then on the "Welcome the New" column.

4. Ask the participants for some conclusion statements—anything they are thinking about, excited about, or worried about. Close with the following comments, and introduce the theme of the prayer that follows:
- You have thought of some wonderful ways to stay connected to your friends, and I am sure you will find new ways as the days and months go by.
- You have also, I hope, begun to think about the new possibilities that will come as you move into a new place in your life.
- Our prayer today will give us an opportunity to acknowledge the sorrow we feel when it is time to say good-bye to people or experiences that we value. We will also pray in thanksgiving for the gifts we have received during our time together.

A Time for Every Season Under Heaven (20 minutes)

Preparation
- Gather the following items:
  - ❏ newsprint, four sheets for each small group
  - ❏ markers, one for each participant
  - ❏ a *Catholic Youth Bible* or other Bible
  - ❏ a prayer cloth (a piece of material that can go on the floor to hold the Bible, candle, leaves, and other prayer materials)
  - ❏ a candle and matches
  - ❏ masking tape
  - ❏ a CD player and a CD of quiet, reflective music (optional)
- Choose a closing song that reflects the theme of friendship or community. Possible song selections can be found in "*Spirit & Song* Connections."

Spirit & Song connections
- "Strength for the Journey," by Michael John Poirier
- "The Call," by Tom Franzak
- "Lean on Me," by Bill Withers

- Cut out copies of the fall and spring leaves found on resource 6, "Seasons' Trees." The fall leaves should be red, yellow, or orange, and the spring leaves should be green. You will need a fall leaf and a spring leaf for each participant.
- Using resource 6, "Seasons' Trees," as a guide, create on separate sheets of newsprint the images of a fall, winter, spring, and summer tree, and hang these on the wall.
- Create a prayer space where the participants will be able to draw or write on the floor and on the newsprint trees that are hung on a nearby wall. Place the Bible, candle, and art supplies (leaves and markers) on a prayer cloth on the floor.
- Invite a participant to proclaim the Scripture reading Eccles. 3:1–8.
- Invite a participant to read resource 7, "Winter Reflection."

Note. If the group is larger than twenty-five people, the activities of this prayer should be done in small groups of about ten.

1. Invite the participants to gather on the floor around the prayer cloth. Begin by asking one of the participants to light the candle.

2. Invite the reader to proclaim the Scripture reading. Allow a few moments for quiet reflection to follow.

3. Ask each of the participants to take a marker from the prayer cloth. Quietly, invite them to go to the summer tree and write on it something they are thankful for about the time they have shared with their friends (laughter, a specific event, shared secrets). You may wish to play instrumental music during this time. When everyone has finished, say:
- Loving God, you have blessed us with (read what is written on the tree). We have great joy in our hearts for the gift that friendship has been in our lives. We thank you and praise you for giving us those moments and for sharing in them with us. We trust that you have been with us all along.

4. Next, invite the participants to take a fall leaf from the prayer cloth. On the leaf, ask them to write the names of the experiences they will miss (core team meetings, retreats, sports practices, and other things they named during the "Ties That Bind" activity). When they are done, invite each individual to go to the fall tree, one at a time, and name one of the things they are going to miss. Have them attach their leaf to the tree, using masking tape. Then say:
- God of fall, we are somehow surprised each year when leaves start to fall from the trees, and yet if we pay attention, we would know that change is constant. Fall helps us to remember that. Be with us today as we mourn a little for the things we will miss—those wonderful things that have sustained us, helped us to grow, and found their way into our hearts.

5. Invite the volunteer to read "Winter Reflection," on resource 7.

6. Pause for a few moments, then invite the participants to offer each other a sign of peace in a unique way. Ask them not to shake hands or hug as they might normally do, but simply to look deeply into each other's eyes. This sign of peace is done in silence—using only the eyes to convey emotions.

7. When all the young people have given each other a sign of peace, say:
- O God of winter, we, like Mary Magdalene, struggle with the challenge of letting go—even when we know that wonderful things are in our future. We want to cling to one another and our experiences, like Mary clinging to Jesus. May we be Easter people too—and trust that in letting go, we are opening ourselves up to good things.

8. Invite the participants to think about the many new and exciting things the future holds. When they are ready, ask them to take a green (spring) leaf from the prayer cloth, and write on it at least one thing they are looking forward to in the coming year. When they are ready, invite them to place their leaf on the spring tree, using masking tape.

9. When all the leaves are on the spring tree, the prayer leader should say the following prayer:
- Creator God, God of spring, and God of all new things, we tremble at the possibilities that lay before us. Like budding trees, we do not really know what the future holds, but we know that our growth cannot be stopped. We trust that you will stand by us through the storms we will encounter, and help us to grow into the people you have called us to be. As we embark on this new season of our life, help us to remember the lessons we have learned, value the experiences that have brought us to this place, and treasure the people who have walked this journey of life with us.

10. Conclude the prayer service with the song that you have chosen.

Options and Actions

- **Celebrate friends.** Invite the participants to write a letter or have conversations with the people with whom they are closest. Ask them to share with their closest friends (or adult mentors) what is most important about the relationship and why they value it so much.
- **Honor experiences.** Invite the participants to reflect on the reasons that the experiences they have celebrated during this session were so important to them. Ask them to consider sharing those reflections with those younger than they are to encourage them to also participate in those experiences.

Family connections

♦ Invite the young people to talk with their parents about their fears and dreams about the future. Invite the parents to also share with their son or daughter their concerns about what the future will hold for their child, and for the relationship between parent and child.

♦ Invite the families to celebrate the ways they have shared faith and life together for the past four years of high school. They might consider creating a scrapbook, spending an evening sharing memories, or even taking a vacation day or two simply to be together.

Media connections

Create a space on a parish Web page where friends can post pictures, messages, and stories in the years ahead. Set up a time, once a month, when the community can gather in a chat room to talk with one another.

Seasons' Trees

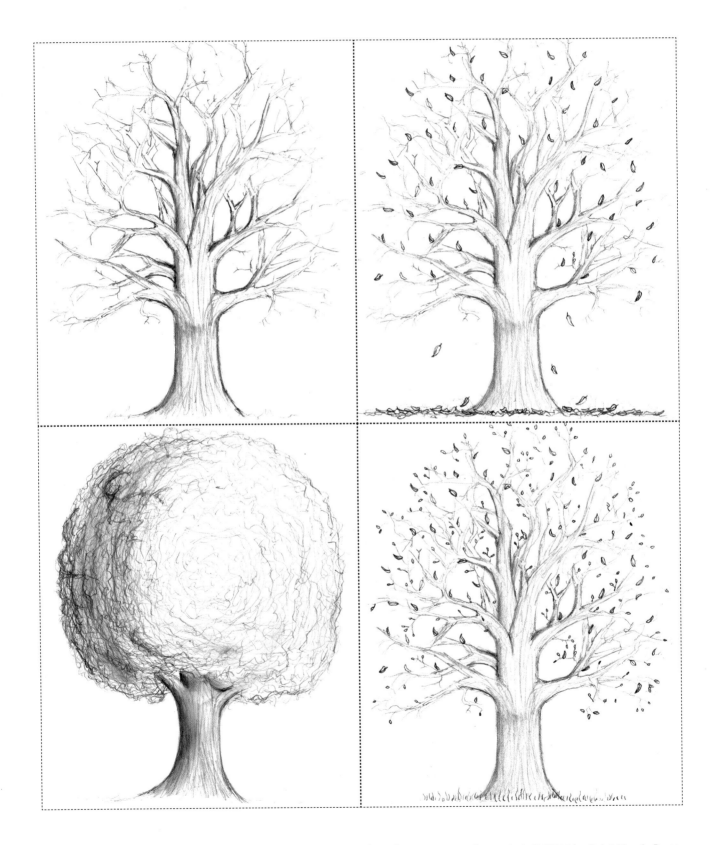

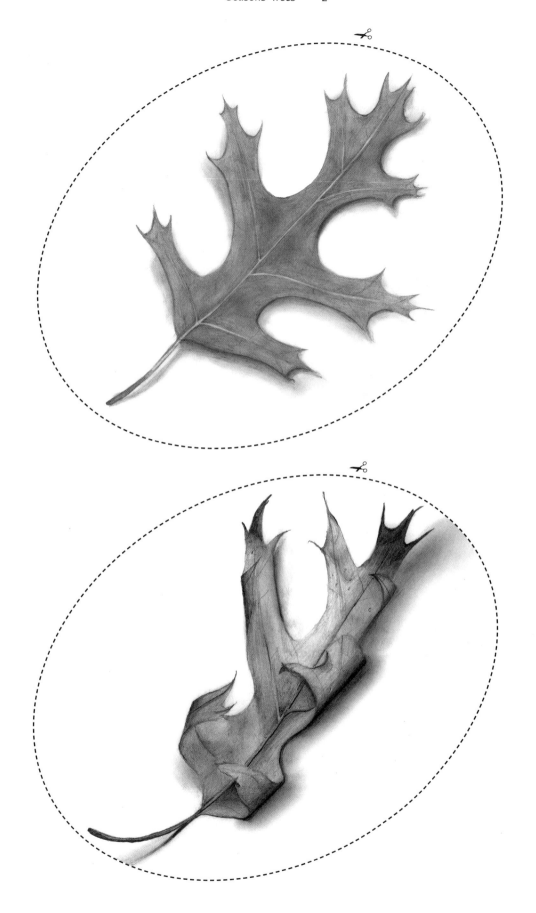

Winter Reflection

The barrenness of winter reminds us that "for everything there is a season." Christians are reminded of this feeling of emptiness each year at Easter when we face again Jesus' death. Being Easter people means that we live in the hope of the Resurrection—knowing that death isn't the end. We can be Easter people at those ending moments too—trusting that it isn't the end, but only a new beginning. Mary Magdalene was at Jesus' tomb after his Resurrection—and when she saw him, she tried to throw her arms around him. Jesus told her, "Mary, do not cling to me!" But to not cling is hard. Perhaps if we could hear Mary Magdalene's heart at that moment, it would sound something like this:

> I never suspected
> > Resurrection
> > > and to be so painful
> to leave me weeping
> With joy
> > to have met you, alive and smiling, outside an empty tomb
> With regret
> not because I've lost you
> but because I've lost you in how I had you—
> > in understandable, touchable, kissable, clingable
> > > flesh
> > > not as fully Lord, but as graspably human.
>
> I want to cling, despite your protest
> > cling to your body
> cling to your, and my, clingable humanity
> cling to what we had, our past.
>
> But I know that . . . if I cling
> you cannot ascend and
> I will be left clinging to your former self
> . . . unable to receive your present spirit.

(Ronald Rolheiser, *The Holy Longing: The Search for a Christian Spirituality* [New York: Doubleday, 1999], page 166. Copyright © 1999 by Ronald Rolheiser.)

Part C
Extended Program

11 Sharing Our Faith:
An Ecumenical Event

Overview

This session is designed to bring cross-denominational conversations and programming to young people. The activities involve youth from different beliefs and faith traditions in learning how to build trust and fellowship with one another. The event gives young people an opportunity to see and celebrate God's activity in all our lives, regardless of denominational affiliation. This event works as an ecumenical event among Christian denominations or with people of different monotheistic faiths (Judaism, Islam, and Christianity). It is essential that those who are leading this event are especially sensitive to the language that is used throughout the event, especially if non-Christian faith traditions are involved.

Outcomes

- The participants will learn about other faith practices and traditions.
- The participants will build community with those from other faith traditions.
- The participants will reflect on their own faith traditions and beliefs.

AT A GLANCE

Sharing Our Faith (4 hours)

- Registration and Opening (30 minutes)
- Events (90 minutes)
  These activities happen concurrently:
  - Faith Bowl
  - Art Project
  - Service Opportunity
  - Human Board Game
  - Coffeehouse
- Break and Setup for Championship Rounds (15 minutes)
- Championship Rounds of "Faith Bowl" (30 minutes)
- Open Mic: Sharing of Faith Traditions (45 minutes)
- Closing Remarks and Prayer (30 minutes)

Pray It

- Opening Prayer (2 minutes)
- Closing Prayer (10 minutes)

Sharing Our Faith (4 hours)

General Preparation Prior to Event
- Several months before this event, you will want to gather a planning team of youth and adults from each faith tradition that is invited to the event. The planning team will need to decide the following:
  - Location, date, and time frame for the event. You will need a location with six breakout rooms and a space big enough to accommodate the whole group.
  - Age range for the event.
- Each church or faith group should take responsibility for one of the tasks listed below, or you may wish to create smaller task groups that include someone from each faith tradition:
  - design and lead the two prayer services
  - design and distribute publicity materials and the registration flyer, collect registrations and fees, establish a budget, and handle the money
  - arrange for snacks or a meal, secure help to serve and clean up
  - organize teams to plan and implement each activity
  - design a welcoming atmosphere, and handle the setup (and cleanup) of the facilities

"Sharing Our Faith" Event Preparation
- For the "Sharing Our Faith" event, gather these items:
  - registration materials: sign-in sheets, nametags, and markers
  - decorations
  - snacks or a meal, drinks, paper or plastic products with which to eat
  - materials listed for the chosen activities
- You will want to review the supplies list for each of the activities listed in this session, and then gather supplies based on the activities you have chosen to conduct.
- You will want to review the directions and steps for each of the activities before the event. Consider conducting a mock event, in which all the activities are tried out by the team beforehand; this will allow you to work out any unforeseen glitches or problems.
- All the activities in the opening event will be happening simultaneously in different rooms or areas. You will want to set up for each activity before the participants arrive.

Registration and Opening (30 minutes)

1. Ask the participants to make a nametag with their name and their faith tradition or church/synagogue written on it. Invite all the participants to sign up for their part in the Faith Bowl game at registration, which is explained in the preparation steps for the Faith Bowl activity.

2. Gather the participants, and welcome them with the following comments:
- Welcome! We are happy that you are here. This is a great opportunity for us to find out more about the different faith traditions that have gathered here today. (You might consider having someone from each faith tradition introduce the name of his or her church or house of worship and the religious tradition to which he or she belongs.)
- It is always a little awkward to be in a group where you do not know people well, so we are going to work together to help you get to know one another better.
- Lots of fun activities are planned to help you find out more about the others in this group, but also to get to know more about what we have in common, and what is unique about us. We trust that you will be open to the others in this room and are interested in knowing more about how we all relate to God.

3. Choose a few large-group community builders, and lead the participants through those activities.

4. Gather the participants together for the opening prayer. Invite the prayer leaders to come forward and conduct the prayer.

5. Go over the following instructions:
- Review the overall flow of the event. You will want to provide an overview of the different activities that are part of the event. If helpful, post schedules (with times and room locations), or distribute them as handouts for the participants.
- Review the schedule for the Faith Bowl activity by letting the participants know when each team is scheduled to participate in this event and by answering any questions.
- Note that the Faith Bowl activity occurs in timed rounds, with time for movement between the rounds. Once the round begins, the door is closed and others are not allowed to enter that activity.
- The other activities are free-flowing; the participants are free to come and go as desired.

6. Invite the first three teams designated for the Faith Bowl to proceed to the game location. All the other participants may choose one of the other activities that will be happening concurrently. Ask them to pick one activity, and proceed to the designated location.

Faith Bowl

Preparation
- Gather the following items:
  - ❏ several pieces of poster board, envelopes, and markers
  - ❏ newsprint sign-up sheets, completed at registration, to be posted outside the Faith Bowl room for reference
  - ❏ a stopwatch or timer
  - ❏ newsprint and markers, or a chalkboard and chalk, to keep track of the scores
- This game is played in the style of *Jeopardy*, although it is not necessary for the questions to be in the form of an answer or the answers to be in the form of a question. The number of categories depends on the number of faith traditions that are participating. Each faith tradition becomes its own category. Before the event ask the leader from each participating faith tradition to provide five questions and answers for the regular round and five additional questions for the championship round. When requesting the questions, ask that they vary in degree of difficulty. Suggest the following categories to help them think of appropriate questions and answers: title or name of clergy, elements of worship, special days or seasons, key elements of their faith tradition, special rituals.
- Make the game board from poster board, listing the categories along the top. Underneath each category, glue envelopes containing the questions to the poster board, and write the point value on the envelope. If the technology is available, this could be done as a PowerPoint presentation and projected onto a screen.
- Create the overall plan for the size of the teams based on those who register for this event and the time you will give to each round. Rounds are 15 or 20 minutes long, with 5 minutes between rounds to move participants in and out of the room. With 20-minute sessions, conduct three rounds; with 15-minute sessions, conduct four rounds. Similar to *Jeopardy*, it works best when three teams participate in each round. Preferably, the teams should consist of six to eight people, but it might be necessary to make the teams larger or to have four teams participate in each round. The teams must have representatives from many or all of the faith traditions. No more than two people of any one faith tradition should be on a team.
- Create newsprint sheets that list the number of teams needed for each round, and indicate places for people to sign up under each team name. For instance, Teams A, B, and C may each have six lines underneath their

title for participant sign-up. These three teams may be participating in the first round of the competition. List the time of the round on the newsprint. As the participants arrive at the event, assist them in signing up to participate in the Faith Bowl.
- A number of leaders are needed to make this successful. An emcee will need to read the questions, at least one team leader will need to determine whose hand is raised first (and second), and one or two additional team leaders will need to serve as scorekeepers.

1. At the start of each round, introduce the way in which the game will be played by explaining the following rules:
- Each team should pick one person to be their spokesperson. This person will raise her or his hand when your group has an answer to the question that is asked. The spokesperson will respond for the group.
- Once a team has been called on, they have 20 seconds to provide an answer.
- If the team is correct, they will get points for that question and will select the next question.
- If the team answers incorrectly, they will lose points for that question, and the other teams will have the opportunity to answer the question in the order that hands were raised.
- The game ends when the time is up. We will be keeping track of the points scored by each team, and the teams with the highest scores will have the opportunity to participate in the championship round.
- We will start by asking Team [name of team] to select the first category.

2. Conduct the first round.

3. When the time for the round is up, announce the scores, and invite the players to depart the room to participate in some of the other activities that are going on elsewhere. Those who will be participating in the championship round are announced just prior to that event.

4. Welcome the next scheduled group for a new game, and play the game by repeating steps 1 through 4.

Art Project

Preparation
- Gather the following items:
  - ❑ supplies as needed for the chosen art project
  - ❑ cleanup supplies
- Decide on the type of project by selecting a theme such as "How I See God." This project is something that all the participants can work on and create together. Following are some ideas:

- ❑ **A banner.** Using felt for the background, provide other materials that the participants can use to create shapes and images on it. Provide material, scissors, glue, and permanent markers.
- ❑ **A graffiti wall.** Use a roll of paper or newsprint sheets taped together to create a backdrop. The participants use markers and crayons to draw, color, and write.
- You will need to have a few team leaders to help the participants with projects and to assure that the designs are appropriate to the event.

Service Opportunity

Preparation
- Gather the following items:
  - ❑ supplies as needed for the chosen service opportunity
- Decide on a type of service opportunity that would benefit a ministry effort from one or all of the faith traditions. The project should be something the participants can work on at this event. Some ideas include:
  - ❑ **Holiday cards or tray favors.** Using art supplies and magazines, the participants can create cards for residents of area nursing homes. Provide construction paper, magazines, old greeting cards, scissors, glue, markers, glitter, and other art supplies.
  - ❑ **Advocacy efforts.** Provide the young people with information about an advocacy effort in your community, nationally, or internationally, such as supporting an environmental effort (water cleanup, endangered animals, or others). The young people can write letters to political leaders or create posters for community display to draw attention to the issue. Provide paper, pens, political leaders' addresses, and a suggested letter format.

Human Board Game

Preparation
- Gather the following items:
  - ❑ supplies as necessary for creation of the game board
  - ❑ hats or bandannas to indicate teams
- Select a game that is active and easy to play (for example, Trouble or Sorry!). Create a life-sized board game using construction paper and masking tape. Tape the game board to the floor. Create oversized dice out of large foam pieces or cardboard boxes. The participants are the game pieces.
- You will need to designate a couple of team leaders, who will oversee the game and introduce new participants into the game as it is being played.

Coffeehouse

Preparation
- Gather the following items (if possible) to create a coffeehouse atmosphere. It might also be possible to find a space in the building being used that would accommodate this activity.
  - ❑ comfortable seating, such as beanbag chairs
  - ❑ beverages
  - ❑ soft lighting
  - ❑ tables
  - ❑ magazines such as *People* or *Seventeen,* Catholic publications such as *Catholic Worker* or *America,* or magazines from other faith traditions
  - ❑ lava lamps (if available)
  - ❑ a CD player and a CD of soft instrumental music
- Create a space that is conducive to conversation and relaxation.
- Invite the adults to talk with and listen to the youth.

Championship Rounds of "Faith Bowl" (30 minutes)

Preparation
- Gather the following item:
  - ❑ a prize for the team with the highest score
- The championship rounds should be held in a space that is large enough so all the participants can watch.
- Select the four teams with the highest score, or select the two teams with the highest scores and the two teams with the lowest scores.
- Use a new set of questions so that no team has an advantage.

    1. Review the rules for the game and answer any questions. Then invite the teams to play the game in the same manner as they did in the previous rounds.

    2. In an effort to engage the audience in this round, be sure to pause after correct answers are given to see if anyone wants to share any additional information about a particular question.

    3. When 30 minutes have passed, the team with the highest score wins and is awarded a prize.

Open Mic: Sharing of Faith Traditions (45 minutes)

Preparation
- Gather the following items:
  - ❑ a microphone and a speaker
- Before the event invite one youth from each of the faith traditions to prepare a 3- to 5-minute summary of their faith tradition. The purpose

---

TryThis

Contract with a coffeehouse in your area to come and sell or donate beverages: smoothies, iced mochas, flavored coffees, tea, and hot chocolate in the Coffeehouse area. If extras such as the beverages are to be sold at the event, be sure this is advertised prior to the gathering.

TryThis

Set up a question box that is available throughout the event. Encourage the young people to write questions they might have about a faith tradition or about the relationship between traditions. If you have time, answer some of the questions during the open mic time. Have the young people put their name and phone number on the question so an adult can follow up with them after the event.

for this faith sharing is to educate, not to evangelize. After each youth has spoken, allow a short time for questions.
- The emcee should introduce each of the young people and facilitate the question-and-answer period.

Closing Remarks and Prayer (30 minutes)

1. Ask the participants to respond to the following two questions:
- What is something you learned today about the other religious traditions?
- What surprised you about what you learned or experienced today?

Drawing on their responses, summarize the event's activities by offering the following comments:
- Our common faith in God (or Jesus, if all are Christian) binds us together. We may have different traditions, beliefs, and styles of worship, but we all believe that we have come from God and are called to live our lives according to God's wishes.
- We hope that you had a chance to learn a little more about the other faith traditions gathered here, and that you have come to know some new people as well.
- We hope we can continue to come together in the future—either in this type of event or perhaps through service opportunities or community projects.
- Let us end this event with prayer.

2. Invite the designated prayer leader or team to come forward and lead the closing prayer.

Prayer is an important part of this event, but it also has the greatest chance of highlighting the differences between the faith traditions. If this event will include people of the Jewish and Muslim faiths, invite representatives from all the faith traditions to plan the closing prayer and to assure that it is appropriate for their participants. The opening prayer is appropriate for all traditions. If the event will include only Christian faith traditions, the closing prayer is offered as a suggestion. It should not be used with non-Christian faith traditions.

Opening Prayer (2 minutes)

Preparation
- resource 8, "Servant of Truth," cut into prayer cards and distributed to each of the participants

1. Invite all the participants to quiet their thoughts and prepare themselves for prayer. You will want to introduce prayer in this way:
- Each of us has learned about God and experienced his presence within our own faith tradition. We know that God is present to each and every one of us. We begin today with a simple prayer that we can be people who bring God into this world through the way we live.

2. Guide the participants in proclaiming the "Servant of Truth" prayer together, as printed on the prayer cards.

Closing Prayer (10 minutes)

Preparation
- Gather the following items:
  - ❑ a *Catholic Youth Bible* or other Bible
  - ❑ a candle and matches
  - ❑ water, in a glass bowl
  - ❑ a table, covered with a cloth
- This prayer service is appropriate for Christian traditions only.
- Invite a participant to light the candle.
- Invite a participant to read "Candle Prayer."
- Invite a participant to proclaim the Scripture reading, Luke 10:25–28.
- Invite a participant to read "Prayer for Religious Dialogue."
- One volunteer from each church community should be invited to say the name of their church (including their denomination if it does not appear in their church name; for example, "Calvary Baptist Church" or "Saint Joseph Catholic Church").
- Choose a song with a water or baptism theme. You'll want to choose something that all the participants know well, or something that can be taught fairly quickly.

1. Gather all the participants together around the prayer table. Invite them to stand.

2. Invite the volunteer to come forward and light the candle while another participant reads the following "Candle Prayer":
- O God, fire is sacred; as we light this candle may we be reminded that we are to burn with the same fire for you. May we fill our lives with that burning love.

3. Invite the reader to come forward and proclaim Luke 10:25–28. Allow a few moments for quiet reflection to follow.

4. Then share the following prayer:
- Jesus, we recognize that we are all neighbors here. We celebrate the good work and faith that each of us brings to our faith communities. We thank

you, God, for . . . (Invite all the churches to stand, one at a time, and state their name.)
- Dear Lord, may we learn to celebrate the many ways you have blessed us and continue to reveal yourself to us. Amen.

5. Standing next to the water bowl, say the following:
- We gather as people who are joined together in Baptism. As a reminder of this gift and of Christ, the living water, we call on the Spirit that lives within this group to bless this water. I invite you to extend your hands over the bowl of water.

Pause as the group extends hands, and then say:
- Creator God, your wonderful gift of water brings life and freshness to the earth. It cleanses all sin and gives us eternal life. We ask you to bless this water and remind us that you are the source of all life and the reason we can call each other sisters and brothers. We ask this through Christ, our Lord. Amen.

6. Invite all the participants to come forward and dip their hands in the water, then to turn around and, with the water, make a cross on the forehead of the next person. You will need to start this process, signing the first person who approaches the table. You may consider playing instrumental music during this time.

7. Invite the second reader to come forward and proclaim the "Prayer for Religious Dialogue," which follows:
- Being of all beings, Lord of all lords, you are the blessed and supreme light of all the peoples of the world. I ask you to bring about a new atmosphere of trust among all the world's religions and cultures. Through our common defense of universal values, foster in us a sincere and conscious search for the things that unite us. Make us instruments of your plan for all people of goodwill and faith to work together in a common effort toward peace.

Source of life and Son of truth, you are the divine and eternal force of all hearts.

We praise you and exalt you for the clear understanding of the interdependence of human beings and nations. We thank you and glorify you for the hope you have instilled in us, and for a world in which respect, liberty, and universal cooperation will reign. Guide and help the work of all people, and especially of religious leaders, as we try to create a path of dialogue among people of all creeds, cultures, and traditions.

(Adapted from "Prayer for Religious Dialogue," in *Prayers of Blessing and Praise for All Occasions,* by Hugo Schlesinger and Humberto Porto, pp. 102–103)

8. Conclude the prayer time by asking the participants to shake hands (or hug), and say, "Peace be with you."

Servant of Truth

My God, I am a servant of your truth;

in my every word and gesture

may my life be a reflection of your love.

I want to spread your life-giving message,

bringing all people to knowledge of you

and awakening in them

a true spirit of community.

Amen.

(Adapted from "Prayer for the Spread of Truth," in *Prayers of Blessing and Praise for All Occasions,* by Hugo Schlesinger and Humberto Porto [Mystic, CT: Twenty-Third Publications, 1987], page 85. Copyright © 1987 by Hugo Schlesinger and Humberto Porto. Used with permission.)

My God, I am a servant of your truth;

in my every word and gesture

may my life be a reflection of your love.

I want to spread your life-giving message,

bringing all people to knowledge of you

and awakening in them

a true spirit of community.

Amen.

(Adapted from "Prayer for the Spread of Truth," in *Prayers of Blessing and Praise for All Occasions,* by Hugo Schlesinger and Humberto Porto [Mystic, CT: Twenty-Third Publications, 1987], page 85. Copyright © 1987 by Hugo Schlesinger and Humberto Porto. Used with permission.)

My God, I am a servant of your truth;

in my every word and gesture

may my life be a reflection of your love.

I want to spread your life-giving message,

bringing all people to knowledge of you

and awakening in them

a true spirit of community.

Amen.

(Adapted from "Prayer for the Spread of Truth," in *Prayers of Blessing and Praise for All Occasions,* by Hugo Schlesinger and Humberto Porto [Mystic, CT: Twenty-Third Publications, 1987], page 85. Copyright © 1987 by Hugo Schlesinger and Humberto Porto. Used with permission.)

My God, I am a servant of your truth;

in my every word and gesture

may my life be a reflection of your love.

I want to spread your life-giving message,

bringing all people to knowledge of you

and awakening in them

a true spirit of community.

Amen.

(Adapted from "Prayer for the Spread of Truth," in *Prayers of Blessing and Praise for All Occasions,* by Hugo Schlesinger and Humberto Porto [Mystic, CT: Twenty-Third Publications, 1987], page 85. Copyright © 1987 by Hugo Schlesinger and Humberto Porto. Used with permission.)

Resource 8: Permission to reproduce for program use is granted. © 2004 by Saint Mary's Press.

Part D
Community-Building Strategies

Creating Community

Five Steps for Community Building

In his book *Building Community in Youth Groups,* Denny Rydberg discusses five steps for building community in groups. A specific process must take place in the life of any group to bring about true community. Before an individual can feel comfortable sharing the joys and struggles of life, he or she must trust the other members of the group. This development of trust and commitment progresses at varying speeds for different people, but all the groups go through the five basic steps outlined below.

Step 1: Getting Started

This first step in community building begins the process of breaking down the barriers that exist among participants. This step always comes first, enabling bonds to be built between the young people.

> This is accomplished by giving the group members some problem-solving tasks which require them to work side by side with others in the group. As they discuss solutions and physically help one another accomplish the goal, bonds are built between people of diverse backgrounds. Cooperation is the main goal. (P. 18)

When young people feel welcomed and have had the opportunity to contribute to a group task, they begin to feel like a part of the group. It is essential that people feel welcomed and accepted in this first step of community building.

Step 2: Opening Up

This step involves young people sharing nonthreatening information about themselves. When they are able to share some simple things, and that information is accepted and welcomed, trust begins to develop. When young people sense (or get specific feedback) that their ideas are not valued or that others do not want to listen to them, trust will not be built and they will not feel like they are a part of the community.

Step 3: Affirming

All of us need to know that others value what we have to say:

> After revealing their inner selves during the opening up step, students need positive feedback to reassure them that others think they are still okay before they will consider sharing further. (P. 19)

This step takes place throughout the community-building process, but it is especially important after personal information has been shared. Many times young people who were reluctant to participate at first will participate with enthusiasm when they realize that others care about them.

Step 4: Stretching

Stretching experiences—planned for or as a natural result of the life of the group—cause a group to express their trust in and commitment to one another in a practical and real way. If a group is together for an extended period of time (months to years), difficult circumstances will arise in the lives of the participants (sudden illness or death, fights between individuals), and the group will struggle to care for each other through their words and actions. This process naturally moves groups to a different level of trust. However, some groups choose to intentionally include stretching experiences in which the participants are forced to work together and rely on each other's strengths. Stretching experiences also create opportunities for tremendous personal growth.

> Facing and overcoming programmed difficulties give students the confidence that they can cope with everyday problems they face. They learn that they can accomplish more than they thought possible. They believe in themselves. (P. 20)

The "laboratory" setting of stretching experiences gives young people a model for facing problems at home, at school, and at work. The positive results from these activities are remarkable as the group members bond together and grow in all areas of their lives.

Step 5: Deeper Sharing

The final step in community building comes when individuals share deeply with other members of the group and set goals. The group "becomes the setting where [youth] can express their inner hurts, visions, and struggles" (p. 21). At this stage they are not condemned or laughed at for their dreams, failures, and hopes for the future:

When a group member shares a problem, the rest of the group is empathetic and gives support and encouragement. The group exists to help the individual talk through possible solutions and set goals. The group holds the individual accountable while giving him or her the freedom to fail. (P. 21)

It is important to develop the ability to assess the trust level in the group, and then to choose community-building activities to match that trust level. Some mistakes would be:

- Asking participants to do too much too soon—not providing for an initial experience within a group that will allow the young people to feel safe and have some fun.
- Asking participants to share important personal information too quickly, before real trust develops. However, it is good to have participants talk about their likes, their dislikes, funny stories from their lives, hopes for the future, and so on. This helps trust to develop.
- Failing to encourage participants to share information and participate in activities. Young people need to know that they are safe in the midst of the community building, and will need to be affirmed for taking the risk to participate.
- Spending too much time doing fun games that are physical and superficial, but never inviting participants to share anything about themselves.

Once group members have developed a strong trust in one another, you should capitalize on that trust by programming opportunities for young people to continue to share at a deep level. Community-building efforts should always move to the next step in the community-buiding process.

One final note about trust building: Community is dependent on relationships of acceptance and trust, and these relationships only develop in small-group or one-to-one experiences. When a large group has a sense of community, that sense of community flows from the interpersonal experiences in smaller groups.

(Information adapted from and excerpts quoted from Denny Rydberg, *Building Community in Youth Groups,* pp. 18–21)

Selecting a Community-Building Activity

Many books devoted to the topic of community building in youth ministry are available. In addition, you will find trade books on building teams, developing leadership, and promoting personal growth with young people. But not every cool idea is a good one, and not every group is ready for even the best community builder. When selecting a community builder, consider the following questions. If you answer yes to any of these questions, you might want to reconsider your choice of community builder.

- ❏ Does the activity belittle or embarrass any person or persons?
- ❏ Is the activity degrading to some persons or a specific group of people?
- ❏ Does the activity give an undue advantage to the brighter, more athletic, or highly skilled person, so that some members of the group will be left out or feel bad about participating?
- ❏ Is the activity sexually suggestive?
- ❏ Will many participants be left out of the activity for a long time?
- ❏ Will some people be unable to participate fully (persons with disabilities, people of various ages, mixed language groups)?
- ❏ Is the activity safe, or can someone be easily hurt?
- ❏ Does the activity seem to create an inner circle of people who are in the know or who will have an unfair advantage?
- ❏ Does the activity ask the group to trust in a situation that is untrustworthy?
- ❏ Does the activity waste food or show a lack of respect for the environment?
- ❏ Does the activity demand a physical closeness that is inappropriate for the level of relationships that are already formed?
- ❏ Does the activity put a lot of attention on the person who is leading the activity, rather than fostering a sense of fun and learning among the participants?
- ❏ Would you dislike participating in this particular activity?
- ❏ Will someone who is overweight be uncomfortable in the activity? Does it draw attention to differences in body structures?

Guidelines to Follow

In selecting appropriate community builders, use the following guidelines for success:
- ❏ The activity is appropriate for the age of the participants.
- ❏ The activity matches the program's goals and complements the components of the program.
- ❏ The connections between the activity and the session theme or topic are easily made.
- ❏ The physical space needed to do the activity is adequate.
- ❏ The participants are dressed appropriately for the activity.
- ❏ The activity is appropriate for the trust level of the group.

Suggestions for Leading Community Builders

There are things you can do to ensure that you provide appropriate leadership for a community-building activity. By paying close attention to the details of the community builder and the following suggestions, you can be assured of success:
- Make sure you really understand the activity. Conduct the activity with a small group of people before leading it at an event.

- Try to understand what is essential in the directions and how you will communicate those essential elements to the participants. Nothing is worse than a 10-minute explanation to a 5-minute game.
- Know when you need everyone's attention and when you do not. If the activity can happen effectively with lots of noise and confusion, then let that happen.
- If the group you are working with is not good at quieting down to listen to directions, do not use activities requiring the constant need to stop and pay attention to a leader. The last thing you want is for a young person's experience of community building to be "the leader yelled at me all night."
- Get all the help that you need. If you have to distribute supplies or get information from the participants, invite volunteers or other leaders to help you. Two minutes of dead time in a community builder can ruin the whole experience.
- If an activity is not working with a particular group, end it quickly.
- It is always good to have a backup plan.
- If you have many leaders facilitating a series of community builders, those who are not leading a particular activity should join in with the participants.

Outline for a Community-Building Event

Resource 9, "Community-Building Event," will assist leaders in planning a night of community building in a parish setting. This can be done within a youth-only gathering or an intergenerational setting. The outline suggests types of activities, and invites you to find appropriate activities in other print resources or through personal experience or creativity.

Community-Building Event

Preparation Steps for a Successful Event
- Practice the community-building activity ahead of time, and become familiar with all dimensions of the activity.
- Review the role of the small-group leaders, and prepare them for their facilitator role.
- Gather all supplies needed for the event.
- Set up the physical space as needed for the selected activities.

Small Groups
If your group has more than ten participants, be sure to include small-group work. The participants can be placed in small groups in many different ways.

Because it is essential that participants feel affirmed for their participation, it will be important to have a trained leader with the small groups. This person sets the tone for how the members of the group will interact with each other, encourages participation, and affirms group members. How will you divide people into groups?

- Plan for small groups:

Welcome
The participants need to know immediately that they are valued and that you are glad they are there. How will you welcome participants? Will you provide name tags?

- Plan for welcome:

Getting-Started Activities

To begin a program, select at least one icebreaker. Icebreakers are team-building activities that often involve physical activity, simple problem-solving activities, and group work.

- Plan for getting started:

Opening Up

Once you have a general level of comfort in the large group, help the participants begin sharing information about themselves. This can be done by having the participants give a verbal response, raise their hand in affirmation of an idea, or move from one side of a room to the other. Another option is for the participants to gather in a small-group setting, and use open-ended sentences, discussion questions, or activities.

- Plan for opening up:

Stretching

Introduce a challenging activity to the participants that requires that they work together to accomplish a task. Trust activities, simulation games, or group puzzles are an effective way to help groups develop a level of trust with one another. It is important to match the activity to the level of trust that you believe will be possible at this point in your event.

- Plan for stretching:

Celebration

Assuming that a group has successfully accomplished a task that involved stretching and growing in trust, celebrate that event! Food, naming the group, prizes, skits, and storytelling about their accomplishments are good ways of celebrating. If the group did not succeed, they may still want to celebrate their attempts.

- Plan for celebration:

Deeper Sharing

By the end of an event, some participants may be ready to share on a deeper level. Other groups may not get to a level of trust that would allow for this deeper level of sharing. Providing opportunities for the participants to share personally with others in the group through small-group discussions, one-on-one conversations, and group activities can be effective with groups where trust has been developed.

- Plan for deeper sharing (if appropriate):

Closing

Close the evening with either the preceding celebration or in some other way, such as extending an invitation to other youth or to intergenerational events happening at the parish, in the community, or at a larger level. Encourage the participants to continue to build community outside of this event. Prayer is an important way to celebrate the community that has been built, and provides a fitting end to the program.

- Plan for closing:

13 Seasonal Suggestions for Community Building

The Fall Season (September, October, November)

Fall means . . . school is beginning, sports are in full gear, crops are being harvested, the weather is changing, new school relationships are developing, and holidays are being celebrated. Ordinary Time in the Church is drawing to a close, and preparation for Advent is anticipated. The fall season provides many opportunities for ministry to happen.

Just for Fun
- hayrides and other fall or harvest events
- fall hikes
- a haunted house or other Halloween-type events
- open gym nights following football games
- community-building nights to welcome new young people

To Help Others
- "Trunk or Treat" night: Parish organizations buy candy for Halloween, and invite neighborhood children to the parish. Representatives of all the parish organizations then hand out candy from a car trunk in the parish parking lot.
- Create a haunted house for the local community. Charge admission to support a local charity.
- Conduct a pumpkin-carving event for the children of the parish. Have older youth help younger children carve their own pumpkins.
- Hold an outdoor lock-in to draw attention to homelessness and to raise money for a local homeless shelter. Consider having a prayer vigil for the entire parish to attend during the event.

- Adopt a school, and collect school supplies at the parish. Have the youth deliver the school supplies and meet the children who will benefit from their generosity.
- Publicize or host a baby-sitting clinic (usually offered by the Red Cross or a hospital) to help prepare young people to become baby-sitters.
- "Rake and Run": Teens go to the homes of elderly people in the community to rake their leaves. They do this anonymously, or leave a note card at the front door that says, "Have a happy day, from the Rake and Run youth group at [name] Parish."

Ideas for Nongathered Activities

- Send prayer cards to the entire parish, asking them to pray for the young people who are in transition—those who are starting at new schools, those who are transferring schools, or those who are starting middle school, high school, or college.
- Send postcards and newsletters to families, letting them know about youth ministry events in the parish and in the surrounding community.
- Create a bulletin board in the parish that celebrates the young people. Include pictures, newspaper articles, posters and details of programs and activities the young people are involved in at school, in the parish, and in the community.

Parish Connections

- On All Souls' Day, invite the members of the parish to remember family and friends who have died. Create a picture wall in the parish in the weeks before All Souls' Day, and invite parishioners to attend the All Souls' Day liturgy in memory of their loved ones. If a young person of the parish has recently died, have her or his friends work together to create a memorial.
- Involve youth in the creation of any parish Thanksgiving food baskets. They can help collect supplies, pack the baskets, and deliver the baskets with the older members of the community.
- Plan a blessing of athletes at a parish liturgy. Invite all the students that participate in football, track, soccer, hockey, and other fall sports to stand and be blessed by the community.
- After Halloween, collect leftover candy from parish families. Use the candy to create study bags for finals week, Valentine treats for a homeless shelter, or for some other use.

Calendar and Community Connections

- Use the Columbus Day weekend to create an extended program: lock-in, fast-a-thon, service project, and so on.

- Invite the whole community to a prayer service at your parish on the morning of football games (or whatever sport is big in your area). Make the prayer service nondenominational, and extend a special invitation to the players, coaches, cheerleaders, marching band members, and their parents. If possible, serve a light breakfast following the prayer service.
- Involve yourself and members of your community in the CROP WALK *(www.cropwalk.org)* or other local events that raise awareness about hunger, illness, or world needs.
- Contact Catholic Relief Services to find resources on addressing hunger and poverty *(www.catholicrelief.org)*.

The Winter Season (December, January, February)

Winter means . . . Advent, the feasts of Christmas, the Holy Family and Epiphany, New Year's Eve, midterm school exams, long hours of darkness (and cold in some places), and the joys of gift giving and receiving. Basketball, hockey, and other winter sports provide many opportunities for ministry.

Just for Fun
- take a ski trip
- go Christmas caroling in the neighborhood
- organize a New Year's Eve party for youth
- attend a Christmas festival, a Christmas light show, or local Christmas events
- sponsor a Valentine's dance
- host a Super Bowl party
- hold a movie night or a game night
- go ice skating as a group

To Help Others
- Host a baby-sitting day for children so their parents can go Christmas shopping.
- Volunteer to baby-sit for parents on Valentine's Day (or on the weekend).
- Host a Christmas dinner dance, inviting adults with developmental disabilities or others who might not have a community with whom to celebrate.
- Go Christmas caroling at a nursing home.
- Decorate for Christmas at a homeless shelter, a women's shelter, or another social service agency.

- Involve your parish in the "Souper Bowl of Caring" *(souperbowl.com)* program.
- Shovel snow for elderly people in the community.

Ideas for Nongathered Activities

- Create study bags for the youth of your parish who will be taking exams. Deliver the goodies to family homes or schools. These study bags can contain a prayer card or handwritten note, candy, pencils, snack food, and other items.
- Create an Advent retreat on the parish Web page, or send it out as an e-mail. The retreat invites youth to read the Scriptures and other reflections, and to think of and pray around the different focuses of the season.
- Connect youth who are interested in specific careers with parish members who work in those areas. Ask the adults to share information about their work via telephone or e-mail, or in person with the young people.

Parish Connections

- Create a take-home kit or conduct a gathered event to help families celebrate Advent.
- Have youth create an Advent wreath for their home. Provide information that can be taken home to help the family use the Advent wreath to pray together.
- Have youth take a special role in the parish's live nativity program. Create a program if you do not have one.
- Involve youth in decorating the church for Christmas.
- Research ways in which other cultures celebrate Epiphany or the feast of the Holy Family. Create an event that centers on those traditions.
- Invite adult members of the parish community to "adopt" children in grades one through eight. The name of the child, the child's address, and the names of the child's parent(s) can be placed on an Advent tree so that adults can adopt a child for the year. Adults should be encouraged to send cards, find out birthdays, and attend plays, games, and other events.
- Add youth to the parish prayer list (perpetual adoration prayer groups, Renew groups, parish petition books, and so on) around exam times. Invite adults to pray for the young people as they prepare for exams.

Calendar and Community Connections

- Use Martin Luther King Jr. Day or Presidents' Day weekend to conduct a lock-in, an extended program, or service programs.
- Participate in your community's Martin Luther King Jr. Day celebrations. If your community does not hold such an event, consider creating one.
- Participate in a winter festival or other winter events in your community.

The Spring Season (March, April, May)

Spring means . . . Lent and Easter, youth involved in plays and orchestras, college applications and entrance exams, spring break, a change of temperature, and graduations. The spring season offers many creative opportunities for ministry to develop.

Just for Fun

- Attend a sporting event—volleyball, softball, baseball—at a local high school, in the community, or for a national sports team.
- Have a "March madness" basketball game night.
- Create a spring break at-home series of events. When other young people are away on trips, gather the young people who have not gone away for fun events each day—bowling, game days, movies, hiking, and so on, or consider scheduling a weeklong service opportunity.

To Help Others

- Clean up your community by sponsoring a garbage pickup and spring cleanup blitz of a community park, a neighborhood, or your parish grounds.
- Volunteer time to help elderly people in the community with household chores, such as cleaning windows, planting gardens, painting, cleaning gutters, and so on.
- Involve your parish in Operation Rice Bowl or Food Fast. Materials are free through Catholic Relief Services *(www.catholicrelief.org)*.
- Help refurbish and repair homes through the Christmas in April® program *(rebuildingtogether.org),* or build homes with Habitat for Humanity International *(habitat.org)*.

Ideas for Nongathered Activities

- Invite adults in the parish to adopt a youth during Lent. Give out the names on Ash Wednesday, and invite the adults to pray for and communicate with the youth during the Lenten season.
- Create an online Lenten retreat program with Scriptures, reflection readings, journaling opportunities, and prayer questions.

Parish Connections

- Invite young people to present a living stations of the cross or Passion play for the parish community.
- Involve young people in Holy Week and Easter liturgies.

- Host family Lenten soup dinners, in which families gather at the parish for a simple meal and prayer.
- Create a parish garden or plant a tree for all those who have passed away in the last year.
- Have a parish rosary during the month of May, or invite families to pray the rosary once a week during May.

Calendar and Community Connections

- Participate in an Italian Saint Joseph's Day table, an Irish Saint Patrick's Day parade, or other event.
- Use the Memorial Day weekend to conduct extended programs.
- Sponsor a Mother's Day retreat, breakfast, or luncheon for grandmothers, moms, and their daughters, children, or grandchildren.

The Summer Season (June, July, August)

Summer means . . . the end of the school year, school exams, swimming, soccer, softball, baseball, track, lots of outdoor activities, summer vacations and time off, traveling, and hot weather. These are more relaxed days, providing time for friends to get together. The summer season provides lots of opportunities for ministry to happen.

Just for Fun

- Spend the day at an amusement park.
- Go to a local community pool, water park, or beach for the day.
- Take a bike ride through a local park, to a specific destination, or as a fund-raiser.
- Offer a prayer service or liturgy at a beach, park, or other outdoor site.
- Go on a hiking or camping trip.

To Help Others

- Have youths volunteer weekly at a community service site, either committing to one site for the whole summer or changing sites each week.
- Have youth participate in a weeklong mission and service program, such as Young Neighbors in Action *(www.youngneighbors.org)*.
- Volunteer with Special Olympics *(www.specialolympics.com)*.

Ideas for Nongathered Activities

- Invite computer wizards to help with the creation of a parish or youth ministry Web site, or use the summer to collect e-mail addresses, and set up weekly or monthly reflections to be sent throughout the year.

- Use the summer to take pictures of all the young people in the parish. Invite the ushers and hospitality ministers to memorize the faces and names of the young people so they can welcome the youth when they arrive for parish liturgies or events.

Parish Connections
- Involve youth in a parish picnic or parish festival.
- Encourage youth to lead and assist with the parish vacation Bible school program.
- Sponsor a Mass for students who are graduating from high school or grade school.

Calendar or Community Connections
- Participate in a Fourth of July community celebration, including fireworks displays, parades, and other patriotic celebrations.
- Sponsor a Father's Day retreat, breakfast, or luncheon for grandfathers, dads, their sons, children, or grandchildren.
- Gather a group and attend a "taste of . . ." event, a community festival, or another summertime event.
- Bring young people who live in the city or suburbs to a family farm for the day. Have them learn about farm life and help with daily chores.

14 Connecting Youth and the Parish

The Importance of Intergenerational Ministry

Long gone are the days when most young people grew up surrounded by extended family, living in tight-knit neighborhoods, and constantly interacting with people of all generations. Today most young people find little opportunity to interact with people outside their own age group, with the exception of adults who have authority over them—parents, teachers, and bosses. Our Catholic parishes may be the only place where teenagers will spend time each week with people of all ages—from the tiniest infant to the eldest member of the community. A great opportunity for intergenerational ministry is built into the structure of our parishes. It allows us to provide young people with mentors, faith guides, and adults who can walk with young people as they grow into adulthood. Additionally, young people have the opportunity within our parish structures to be guides to those who are younger than they are, as well as to provide insight and talent to the whole parish and its leadership. In *Renewing the Vision,* the U.S. Catholic bishops say:

> Ministry with adolescents recognizes the importance of the intergenerational faith community in sharing faith and promoting healthy growth in adolescents. Meaningful involvement in parish life and the development of intergenerational relationships provide young people with rich resources to learn the story of the Catholic faith experientially and to develop a sense of belonging to the Church. Ministry with adolescents can incorporate young people into the intergenerational opportunities already available in the parish community, identify and develop leadership opportunities in the parish for young people, and create intergenerational support networks and mentoring relationships. Age-specific programs can be transformed into intergenerational programming and new intergenerational programs that incorporate young people can be developed. (P. 22)

Youth ministry programs can enhance the intergenerational opportunities available within the parish in many ways. The following four approaches will help you to begin:
- Infuse intergenerational relationships and programming into the existing youth ministry program and activities. Redesign youth-only events to include other generations, create mentor relationships for youth, and create activities and projects that invite young people to tap into the wisdom of other generations.
- Incorporate youth into the ministries and leadership roles of the parish community. Invite youth into parish leadership, create new roles for young people within the parish, and invite youth to learn about parish ministry through apprenticeships.
- Align youth ministry programming with the life and events of the parish community. Help young people participate in and take leadership for the weekly liturgy, special liturgies, the sacraments, and other parish programs such as service projects and parish community events.
- Create new models of intergenerational programming. Find new ways for youth to interact with the generations, including social events, intergenerational music events, and learning opportunities.

Ideas for Making Parish Events More Youth Friendly

If you are not a coffee drinker, you probably know the experience of attending a meeting or event where the only beverage served is coffee. The question asked is, "Would you like a cup of coffee?" not "Would you like something to drink?" As a non-coffee drinker, you are left with the choice of either not having anything to drink or apologetically asking for something that is not offered. If a parish is not attentive to the needs of young people, the young people can find themselves in a similar situation. They must either live without the opportunity to participate fully in the life of the parish, or they must ask for their needs to be meet.

In *Renewing the Vision,* the U.S. Catholic bishops say, "If parishes are to be worthy of the loyalty and active participation of youth, they will need to become 'youth-friendly' communities in which youth have a conspicuous presence in parish life" (p. 13).

Youth-friendly parishes welcome young people into their midst and support them with time, facilities, and money. They see young people as resources, and empower their gifts and talents. Youth-friendly parishes also provide young people with opportunities for intergenerational relationships. To become youth friendly, a parish first needs to "weed out" practices that judge or isolate youth. A second step is to make youth feel welcome, comfortable, involved, and included throughout the following areas of parish life:
- Community life: parish festivals, hospitality times, parish picnics
- Worship: liturgies, prayers of the community

- Justice and service: ongoing service involvement, justice education, advocacy efforts
- Faith formation: whole-parish learning experiences, catechetical programs

For each area of parish life, ask the following questions:
- Do we need to eliminate anything (activities or attitudes) that might make youth feel unwelcome or uncomfortable?
- In what ways can we intentionally welcome youth?
- How can our parish planning always keep young people in mind?
- How can we begin to mentor and involve youth in leadership, planning, and evaluation?

The following are some ideas that will help you make your parish events more youth friendly.

Food

Take a close look at what is being served. Is anything available that young people will eat? If you are not sure about what they might want to eat, ask them! At "coffee and donut" gatherings, make sure juice or soda is available. At evening meetings, be sure soda, bottled water, or other cold beverages are available. Be attentive to the fact that many young people run from one activity to the next. They might arrive at an evening meeting right from a sports practice. Something as simple as a bowl of pretzels will keep their stomachs from growling and their attention on the important issues.

Time

Young people often have more on their calendars than adults do. They come home from school with hours of homework. They participate in after-school activities, play on sports teams, play in a band, serve in leadership roles at school, in the parish, and in the community, and often work at a part-time job. When scheduling activities and meetings, keep those schedules in mind. Daytime meetings—during school hours—automatically exclude young people. However, young people would be available on days when there is no school (holidays, teacher conference days, and school breaks). If a group needs to meet during the day, look for a day when young people are not in school. Some young people are not involved in after-school activities, and they are available in the late afternoon for meetings or activities, and Sundays seem to be a time when fewer young people are involved in activities and job responsibilities.

Transportation

Not all young people have easy access to transportation. If youth are participating in leadership roles alongside adults, ask the adults to provide transportation for the young people. Give careful consideration to ensuring the safety of the young people by following parish and diocesan policies.

Behavior

Young people are not mini-adults. They are in the midst of a tremendous growth spurt, and they are changing every day. Adults who work with young people know that a young person may not always know the right way to behave, the best way to communicate information, or even something as simple as the appropriate way to dress for an occasion. Often this is not a sign of rebellion but rather a sign of immaturity. Adults help adolescents learn the information or skills they are lacking by quietly addressing concerns with the young person in an honest, up-front, and respectful manner.

Physical Needs

Only infants experience a greater change in their bodies than do adolescents. For younger adolescents, they may be physically unable to "sit still." Their bodies are growing so quickly that they experience restlessness, physical pain, and other sensations that make it impossible for them to sit for long periods of time. Simple things like stretch breaks are good for everyone, but they are essential for young people. In parish activities it is not uncommon to find a group of middle-school children chasing each other through the parking lot or the parish center. Although the safety of all is of primary concern, can you find places and times when young people can be allowed this energy release?

Youth Representation

If a young person cannot find anyone like them who is involved in parish activities, they assume that they are not a part of the community. When evaluating your parish liturgy and liturgical events and other parish functions, look at the event through the eyes of a young person. If no young people are involved in leadership at an event, the message communicated is that young people are not important. If it is obvious that the event does not welcome teenagers, we should not be surprised when they do not participate.

Parish Events That Bring Generations Together

In a youth-friendly parish, the generations come together naturally throughout parish life. Being intentional about the process of becoming youth friendly means including youth in all the ongoing aspects of life as a parish. It can also include creating some new traditions together. Consider the following ideas for bringing the community together.

Celebration of the Saints

This event consists of a reception that is held after a Sunday liturgy (or an All Saints' Day liturgy). The activity could be prepared by young people but would involve the entire parish in celebrating the many cultures that make up the Church. Set up a table for each of the cultures, and include the following items:

- a picture or statue of a saint from a particular cultural community
- a poster describing the life of the saint and the way in which he or she lived the life of Christ
- information about the culture of the saint (for example, maps, a list of the values of the community, pictures of families from the culture, stories of migration to the United States)
- cookies or snacks from the culture

Senior Prom

This event brings the senior citizens of the parish together with young people. The young people host a Senior Prom, inviting all those who are over the age of sixty to participate. Follow these guidelines to make the event a success:

- Send out personal invitations to all the seniors in the parish, including an invitation to parish groups that primarily involve seniors. Invite the seniors (and youth) to dress up. If you can arrange for chauffeurs (parents or older teens) to pick up the seniors, attendance will be much higher.
- Host the event free of charge or at a low cost. Invite the parents to cook the meal and the youth to provide desserts. Decorate the parish center, and use a quality sound system. Select music that seniors will enjoy dancing and listening to, and ask some seniors for help in choosing songs.
- Ask a local florist to donate corsages and boutonnieres for all the seniors who attend.
- As the hosts for the event, the young people invite the seniors to dance, or sit and visit with them if they are not interested in dancing. Ask a few young people to lead community dances such as the Hokey Pokey, the Chicken Dance, or the Electric Slide. Invite the seniors to teach the young people their dances—a waltz, swing dancing, or the fox trot.
- Get a young person or a parent to serve as the official photographer for the night, complete with a backdrop. Publish the picture on a bulletin board at the church, and send a copy to all the seniors who participated.

Discovering the Story of Our Parish

Invite a group of young people to research the history of the parish. This research can be done by examining church and diocesan records. An interactive approach would include talking with older members of the parish. Look for the following information:

- How was the church established? In what year and place? What has changed since then?
- How was the site selected or acquired?
- How was the name chosen?
- When was the church building erected? If there are other church buildings, when were they erected?
- How big was the parish at the beginning? How is it different now?

Once the information has been gathered, sponsor a "birthday party" for the entire community, where the story can be told and pictures, building plans, and membership lists can be displayed. Include any original parishioners (or lifelong members) as guests of honor.

Knowing the Generations

Invite a group of young people to interview members of the community. Create a list of interview questions, and find out as much as possible about the older generations in the parish community. The young people can ask about:

- the names, occupations, and countries of origin of their parents and grandparents
- their early school days (what was it like to be a teenager when they were young)
- how they met their spouse, chose their occupations, or discerned their vocations
- the places they have lived—different countries, states, cities, or houses and apartments
- wars or historical events they participated in or remember

When the interviews are done, create an article for a parish newsletter or a bulletin board display to help others know about these parishioners. Or host a dinner or a parishwide reception for the interviewees. Invite the young people to share the story of the person they interviewed through stories and pictures.

Peer Mentors for New Members:
Guardian Angel Program (GAP)

Program Overview

The Guardian Angel Program (GAP) is one strategy you can use to encourage ninth-grade youth to participate in the parish youth ministry program. GAP provides an opportunity for welcome and outreach to those who are just starting high school, and supports their participation in a high-school-level youth ministry program. Older youth maintain contact with the ninth-grade students, and are their "guardian angels" when they attend activities. The program's success depends on the willingness of the older youth to befriend the ninth graders of the parish. This is best accomplished with a core team of students who are regular participants.

- A GAP team of tenth to twelfth graders is formed. The team's job is to invite, welcome, and befriend ninth graders (and new high-school-age parishioners).
- Each GAP team member is assigned approximately five ninth graders, and is expected to be in contact with each of them on a regular basis (at least four times during the school year).
- The GAP team coordinator meets with the team regularly to provide training and mentoring to the team and to ensure that all members are meeting their GAP team responsibilities.

For the Coordinator

It is the responsibility of the coordinator of the GAP team to invite and prepare the young people who will serve on the team, to oversee their work, and to handle the necessary preparation steps. The coordinator will be responsible for the following tasks:

- Compile a complete list of the incoming ninth-grade class by consulting parish records—school records, religious education records, and the parish census. You will want to have each young person's address, phone number, and e-mail address. In addition, as new young people join the parish, they should be assigned to a GAP team member.

- Communicate with the parents of the ninth graders during the summer to let them know about the Guardian Angel Program. Ask them to encourage their ninth grader to become involved in the youth ministry program. Ask permission to distribute family information, such as phone numbers, e-mail addresses and home addresses, to the members of your GAP team.
- Invite a team of high school youth (in grades ten through twelve) who will commit to the program and the necessary training and mentoring that are involved. These youth should be accepting of others, and willing to befriend ninth graders.
- Assign the GAP team members to the ninth graders. Be attentive to this matching. You may want to assign someone of the same gender to each ninth grader. Additionally, you may wish to assign youth by matching the schools they attend, geographic neighborhood, or other appropriate criteria.
- Provide training for your GAP team (see the following section, "GAP Team Training and Orientation," for some training ideas).
- Meet regularly with the GAP team to review their participation as team members. Keep track of the GAP team by checking in with them regularly. Ask questions such as: How are you doing? What seems to be working well? What struggles are you having? Clarify any rules or safety issues. You will want to use your GAP team meetings to continue to train and mentor youth on ways to be welcoming, encouraging, and hospitable. Review the progress of the ninth graders' participation in the youth ministry community.
- Assign a new GAP team member to the ninth graders if a GAP team member drops out of the ministry or is not performing her or his duties (after attempting to intervene and get the young person involved more fully). Make sure all ninth graders get the support they need from their GAP team member.
- Evaluate the program throughout the year, and conduct a thorough evaluation with the GAP team and some of the ninth graders at the end of the school year.

GAP Team Training and Orientation

To ensure the team's commitment, make sure you conduct an extended orientation and training session. Some ideas for this session include:
- Discuss the following questions with your GAP team:
  - How did you feel when you arrived at your first high school youth ministry event?
  - What did people do that made you feel welcomed?

- What did people do that made you feel left out?
- When did you start feeling comfortable attending the youth ministry programs?

From this information, invite the GAP team members to create a list of do's and don'ts for welcoming new people into the youth ministry community. Use this list as a way to help the GAP team understand what they should and should not be doing.

- Provide the team members with a copy of handout 6, "GAP Team Responsibilities." Take time to review the job description in its entirety, allowing for discussion as needed. Also be sure to allow time to answer any questions the team members might have.
- Talk with the GAP team about their important role in welcoming and connecting new people to the youth ministry community. Say something like the following remarks:
  - Because of the work you do, the ninth graders should have an easier transition into our youth ministry and their high school, and the parish will have the unique opportunity to welcome their gifts and talents. This ministry of welcome is a unique privilege, and you play an important role. The Catholic Church should always be reaching out and welcoming people. Your ministry welcomes young people into our youth ministry efforts, where they can continue to grow in faith.
- Talk with the young people about the importance of reaching out and not being exclusive, with comments similar to these:
  - Because your role is ongoing and primarily one of welcome, the GAP team has to be careful not to be seen as a closed group or a clique. Nothing will turn people off more than if the GAP team is seen as unwelcoming and closed.
- Review with the team any safety issues, diocesan policies, and parish policies that are important to this program. You may wish to consider the following:
  - Does parish or diocesan policy allow a GAP team member to drive his or her ninth graders to and from events?
  - What happens if a ninth grader shares information about abuse, suicidal thoughts, or the like. How should the GAP team member handle these situations? Who should be informed? How? When?
  - If a GAP team member discovers information about his or her ninth graders' participation in dangerous activities (drinking, sexual activity, destruction of property), how should the team member handle the situation? Who should be informed? How and when?

You may want your GAP team to acquire and practice many skills throughout the year, and the Total Youth Ministry resources can be of great assistance to you, in particular *Ministry Resources for Youth Leadership Development*.

Ongoing GAP Team Ideas

Consider the following strategies and ideas for enhancing your ministry to and with ninth graders and new members:

- At gathered events, give special recognition to ninth graders who are present. Their GAP team member can introduce them.
- Create GAP welcome bags, and deliver them to the homes of the ninth graders prior to the first school-year youth ministry program. Include information about the youth ministry program, a top-ten list of reasons to participate, a list of do's and don'ts for high school, a free-entrance coupon for an upcoming event that has an admission fee, and so on.
- Schedule a "GAP only" event that is hosted by the GAP team and is specifically for the ninth graders.
- Begin a GAP prayer chain, in which the team will pray for the concerns of the ninth graders they have adopted. Use the liturgical seasons (for example, Advent, Lent, All Saints' Day) as connecting points with the ninth graders.

GAP Team Responsibilities

First Contact

1. Before the start of the school year, contact each of your ninth graders by phone. After introducing yourself, initiate a conversation about high school and about the high school youth ministry program. You should also introduce yourself to his or her parent(s). Following are some possible questions to use:
- Which high school are you attending?
- How are you feeling about your first day of school?
- Do you have any questions that I could answer for you (either about the specific school or about the high school experience in general)?
- Are you familiar with our high school youth ministry program?
- Let me tell you a little about the program. (Then follow with details of upcoming events and why you are involved. Extend an invitation to the young person to participate in an upcoming youth ministry activity.)

2. Tell the ninth graders that you are a member of the GAP (Guardian Angel Program) team, and that you would like to maintain contact with them throughout the year. Ask them if it would be okay if you contacted them every month (or two) to see how they are doing with school and to tell them about upcoming youth ministry programs and events. If they say yes, make sure the phone number and e-mail address you have for them is correct, and ask the best way to contact them.

3. Let your ninth graders know that you would be happy to meet them at youth ministry events and "show them the ropes." Ask if they are willing to meet you at an upcoming event. If they say yes, schedule a time and place to meet.

4. Give the persons you are sponsoring your phone number and e-mail address, and invite them to contact you if they have questions about youth ministry, high school, or anything else they think you might know about.

Maintaining Contact

Establish ongoing communication with the ninth graders you are sponsoring in the following ways:
- At least once a month, send information to the persons for whom you are responsible. This can be done with postcards designed by the GAP team or through e-mail.

- At least once a season (summer, fall, winter, and spring), call your ninth graders. Find out how they are handling the transition to high school, and encourage their participation in the youth ministry program.

Newcomers at Youth Ministry Events

When a new person arrives at a youth ministry event, you should:

- Welcome the young person. If you are not their GAP team member, find the person who is. If that person is not there, be a stand-in for the night.
- Introduce the young person to other GAP team members, other ninth graders, and the other participants. Be sure to introduce the ninth grader to the adults who are present.
- Stay by the side of the new person. You will want to explain anything that might be confusing to a new person (prayer styles, activities that are used often in youth ministry, the style of meetings or making decisions, and other things). One of your jobs is to make sure the person doesn't feel left out. Sometimes this happens because new people don't understand a group's "rules"—those unwritten ways in which groups behave and relate to one another. You will need to be the interpreter for the night.
- Invite her or him to come to the next activity, and arrange to meet the young person at the activity, if possible.

Other Responsibilities of Gap Team Members

- Be welcoming at all times and in all places, not only when they are "on the job." This includes at school and at school activities, in the neighborhood and in public places, and especially at church (including parish liturgies, youth ministry activities, parish events, and so on).
- Work at remembering names and faces, so that someone who comes to an activity or event for a second or third time can be greeted by name.
- Ensure that you don't become a clique by being careful not to congregate as a GAP team, to the exclusion of others, during events.

16 Promoting Positive Behavior in Community

Some Basic Rules

Young people are known for testing boundaries, but they are testing them specifically to find out what is acceptable and allowed. Communities with strong behavioral boundaries show young people how to act and provide them with a feeling of safety. Adults have a profound impact on the way communities create and live within boundaries.

Discipline, and all the other ways we promote positive behavior, plays an important role in community. How young people relate to one another and how adults treat them has a profound impact on a community. When a common understanding of appropriate behavior exists within a group, and each individual is held responsible for his or her behavior, trust develops and community flourishes.

The strategies listed here assist youth ministry leaders in creating healthy groups and ensuring the safety—physical, spiritual, and emotional—of the young people in their care. To use these strategies successfully, all adults who work in the youth ministry program will need to have a common understanding of the ways in which positive behavior can be promoted. Permission to reprint the following information is granted. You will want to provide copies of these strategies to each of the adult leaders, as well as opportunities to identify, discuss, and clarify ways in which the team can implement these strategies.

Be a Model

Everything we do communicates something to young people. Adults must be vigilant about their own behavior. Adults who swear, smoke, make fun of people, ignore a rule, or forget to clean up after themselves give young people permission to do the same. Adults must live according to the same rules of behavior we expect young people to adhere to.

Be Concerned About All Types of Behavior

The "treat each other with respect" rule is just as important as the "no drinking" rule. All young people, indeed all people, have a right to physical, spiritual, and emotional safety.

Hold Participants Accountable for Their Behavior

Create a covenant with the participants at the beginning of events, or create a yearlong agreement for behavior. Post the covenant, and include it with all event information. Talk about the consequences of violating the covenant. Remind youth and adults that the community depends on the willingness of each person to live by the covenant. Encourage everyone to see the covenant as an agreement about how they want to be in relationship with one another.

Use Times When Rules Are Broken as Learning Experiences

Rules will be broken—intentionally or without thought. When rules are broken, talk with the young people (either the whole group or individuals) about the importance of community and the ways rules help communities build a foundation of trust.

Address Concerns When They Happen

When someone misbehaves, stop the behavior right away. When leaders allow bad behavior to continue for a long time, that behavior becomes a community norm, and it is difficult to bring about change. If young people are talking when they should be listening, pause and ask for quiet. If youth are taking more than their share of food during snack time, ask them to leave the snack area or to put some food back. If a few people are making fun of someone, pull them aside immediately, and discuss with them the inappropriateness of their behavior. Set the boundaries for behavior early and often! It is important to do this in a way that will not humiliate young people.

Give Adults Responsibility for Enforcing the Rules

Young people will test adults to find out who will let them get away with what. The adult who has the lowest standard for behavior will provide the standard that the young people will follow. Work with the adults to ensure that they all know the rules and standards of behavior and can agree to a common method for dealing with problems.

Make Adults a Part of the Community

In youth ministry, whether you are making a decision about where to eat or negotiating a bedtime, adults need to have a voice in the decision—after all, the decision affects them too. Adults may bend to the desires of young people (pizza again!), but must strive not to set up an us-versus-them attitude. When talking about the "we" of a group, make sure everyone knows that "we" includes both the young people and the adults.

Honor the Chain of Command

Young people need to know that some decisions are not up for negotiation, and adult volunteers need to know that they must honor the role of the coordinator of youth ministry. Try to communicate honestly about who has the final authority in decision making.

Encouraging Positive Behavior

Get the Adults on Board

Have a clear vision for how you want young people to interact with one another and how adults will interact with them as well. Communicate that vision to all the adults who work in the youth ministry program. Be specific about the types of behavior that are not tolerated and how misbehavior should be handled. Be specific about the positive behavior you are hoping to foster, and be consistent and clear about your standards.

Have a Positive Attitude About Behavior

Assume that young people really do know how to behave, and communicate through your words and actions that you believe they are capable of following some basic rules and treating one another well. Catch young people doing good things, and make an example of them. Give as much attention to good behavior as you do to bad behavior.

Create a Positive Atmosphere

Use your own energy and love of young people to create an atmosphere in which participants feel loved and respected. Listen to them, encourage them, and be attentive to their needs. When young people feel valued, they are more likely to honor the rules of behavior you are promoting.

Let Your Faith Be Seen

To teach Gospel values of peace, acceptance, forgiveness, and love, we must live those values in our everyday interactions with one another. When talking about rules of behavior, ground those rules in our understanding of

Christian community. Proclaim those values by the way you interact with young people.

Involve the Participants in Community Decision Making

When decisions need to be made, such as renegotiating a lights-out time or deciding what to do when a planned speaker doesn't show up, ask the participants for input or have the whole group (youth and adults) make the decision. When young people are invested in the decisions that are made, they take their responsibilities seriously, and will most often act in the best interest of the group.

Teach About Community

Young people need to learn that what is best for them as an individual may not always be best for the community. When a young person complains at an overnight event that they cannot fall asleep without music playing, she or he needs to know that others may not be able to fall asleep *because* music is playing. Helping young people recognize that their behavior has consequences for others invites them to think about the needs of the group when they are making decisions.

Dealing with Problems

Be Clear About the Problem

Telling a young person to stop talking may not be enough. Let that young person know how his or her talking is affecting the group and the leaders. Be clear when dealing with a problem. Explain that you are concerned with what is best for all who are involved. Whenever possible, invite the young people to contribute more positively to the group by appealing to the gifts and talents you have seen in them.

Know When to Deal with Problems Privately or Publicly

Taking a young person aside and privately explaining your concerns to her or him is the best way to handle some problems. This allows the young person to deal with you directly, away from the eyes and ears of her or his peers. Other times, however, it is best to be public in your disapproval of an action (not a person), so that everyone can learn what is and is not appropriate. Be careful not to humiliate a young person in the process of addressing issues publicly. If you find that a young person has become embarrassed or humiliated, address the issue with her or him privately, and apologize for your role in embarrassing her or him.

Know When to Deal with Individuals or with the Group

At times it will be obvious that a few young people have taken it upon themselves to ignore the rules and disregard the rest of the community (for example, when young people are caught drinking or an individual makes fun of someone). In those cases, deal with the individuals apart from the whole group. At other times, however, the entire group should be asked to address the problems caused by a few. This method works when you do not know who was involved or if it is obvious that some members of the group ignored the behavior of their peers. In those instances the goal is for the whole group to deal with the problem and come up with solutions or consequences.

Be Honest

If trust has been broken or if you are disappointed, communicate that to the young people. However, it is important to remember that it is difficult to be both angry and honest at the same time. When we are really angry, our emotions take over, and we tend to exaggerate. If you are too angry to deal with the situation, ask someone else to do it, or walk away until you can get control of your emotions. Anger can make a bad situation worse.

When dealing with a problem situation within a group, use the following suggested outline for the conversation:

- *Be as clear as possible* about the behavior you have witnessed and why it is inappropriate. Be honest about your emotions or your reaction to the young people's behavior.
- *Get some insight* into or an explanation for their behavior.
- *Be patient* when waiting for the young people to respond. Listen carefully to the answers, and reflect back what you are hearing from them.
- *Invite the young people to consider the consequences* of their actions. This is an important step, because both short-term and long-term consequences affect not only their group but other groups as well. They need to recognize that personal behavior has societal consequences.
- *Ask the young people* what they should do to correct the situation.
- *Affirm them in taking responsibility* for their actions. Find a way to assure the young people that you still value them and love them, even though you are disappointed with their behavior.

If the young people have not taken responsibility for their behavior and the consequences it has brought, it might be appropriate to take further action. Calling parents or the pastor, ending the activity early, or changing the rules for the event may be necessary. You want to give the young people every chance to learn from the situation and grow, but if they are not receptive, do not proceed as though they are.

Practical Jokes

Too often adults either look the other way when young people are involved in practical jokes or, worse, are involved in the pranks themselves. People often believe that practical jokes are a way of building community, but they actually do the opposite. Although the jokes can be funny at first, most often they lead to an escalation of pranks that produce hurt feelings, destroy property, and cause young people to disregard community rules.

When young people are forced to focus their energies away from practical jokes and into positive ways of interacting, they find a greater opportunity to build meaningful and lasting relationships with their peers and with the adults of the community. Here are some ways of avoiding or dealing with practical jokes and pranks:

- Adults should never be involved in leading or suggesting practical jokes.
- At the start of an extended event, tell the young people that practical jokes are not allowed. Explain how practical jokes actually hurt people's feelings and destroy property.
- At the first sign of a practical joke, put a stop to it.
- If pranks or practical jokes have gotten out of hand, sit the group down and talk about what you are seeing. With a little honesty, the group should be able to name uncomfortable feelings and realize that time is being wasted. If the group is not able to name those issues, the adults should name them for the young people.
- If practical jokes continue, call the young persons' parent(s) and send them home from the event. Arrange to meet with the young people and their parent(s) to discuss the incident. As with all situations of this type, the young people should know that they are welcome to attend future events if they are willing to follow the rules of the community.
- If young people are talking about practical jokes when telling stories of school or other events, try to use that moment to help them see how practical jokes are not good things.

Creating a Behavioral Covenant

Whenever a group of young people is going to be together for an extended period of time, it is appropriate to create a covenant with them. This can include yearlong programs (religious education classes, peer ministry groups), extended events, or one-day programs.

The use of the term *covenant* connects with the type of agreement God made with the Israelites in the Old Testament. A covenant is a sacred promise made between people. A covenant is also a set of rules for behavior that all members of the community agree to live by. The young people and adults have a say in which rules are to be part of the covenant.

To create a covenant with a group, invite all the young people and adults to gather in a common space. You will need newsprint, markers, and masking tape. It is important that everyone has input into the covenant. Use the following process:

- Invite the participants to answer the following question: What should be true about how we live together (for the next few hours, days, or year)? Post this on newsprint.
- Ask if any specific rules would need to be followed for the things listed on the newsprint to happen. Post those rules on newsprint.
- Ask if any other rules should be on the list—rules that will ensure the safety of everyone. Add those to the newsprint.
- Invite the participants to think about appropriate consequences for breaking the rules. Post the consequences on a new sheet of newsprint. Assess which consequences are appropriate for which rules.
- When everyone has had the opportunity to talk about the rules and the consequences, and they have all been listed on newsprint, ask if everyone is able to live with the rules and consequences. If necessary, make appropriate changes.
- You might wish to add items to the list, specifically if the young people have not provided a lot of rules or consequences. The following three ideas are helpful for any community:
  ○ Everyone should be open to the other people in the group, to the new experiences they will have, and to changes they may experience within themselves.
  ○ Each person should be honest in his or her words and actions.
  ○ Everyone should be respectful of the other people, the facility, and the rules.
- Ask everyone to sign the covenant as an agreement that they are willing to live by the rules and accept the consequences.
- Keep the covenant posted in a public area, and refer back to it if problems arise.

17 Making the Most of Extended Events

Travel Ideas

Getting to and from actual events or experiences should always be considered a part of the journey. Giving attention to what happens "on the way" will make every event stronger. Consider some or all of these ideas:

- Create a puzzle book that youth can work on as individuals or in teams. Give prizes to the first person or team that solves each page. Use different types of puzzles (word searches, crosswords, brainteasers, and others), so everyone can find something they like to do.
- If you are traveling by bus, create times during the ride when the participants will be involved in intentional sharing. After each break ask people to sit next to someone they don't know, and provide two or three questions for them to talk about.
- Use *The Book of Questions,* by Gregory Stock (Workman Publishing Company, 1987), or make up your own list of questions to start car or van conversations. Be careful to choose questions that are appropriate for a Catholic group of youth to talk about.
- If your group is traveling in different vehicles, invite the participants to change vehicles at each stop. If you are traveling for several days, rearrange the seating every day.
- If the vehicle has a VCR or a DVD player, use it to show a movie that will lead to an interesting conversation. Do not play endless videos, however; allow time for quiet conversations.

Prayer and Liturgy

Extended events provide unique opportunities for young people to engage in extended prayer times. Use the following ways to pay close attention to prayer on extended events:

- Take significant amounts of time out of your schedule for prayer. Plan to spend at least an hour a day in group prayer.

- Schedule private, silent prayer within the context of the experience. For example, gathering participants around a campfire can accomplish this during fun experiences. Journaling offers another unique opportunity for quiet prayer. Give the participants 15 to 60 minutes simply to reflect on the day.
- Visit sacred places, such as churches or shrines, on your way to other activities. Use these moments for prayer or liturgy.
- Invite young people to lead prayer or to give witness talks during prayer.
- Create interesting and engaging prayer that draws on the immediate environment. If you have access to the outdoors, pray there. If you are involved in a mission experience, pray in that location.
- Offer a grace before all meals, start and end the day with prayer, and celebrate the Eucharist when possible.
- Introduce various prayer forms to the youth—meditation, contemplation, centering, morning and evening prayer, Eucharistic adoration and devotions, Scripture reflection, journaling, and other unique prayer opportunities.

Building Relationships with Adults

Adults have a unique opportunity to get to know young people during extended events, but it is equally important that young people get to know adults in a more personal way. Pay attention to these opportunities.

- Extended events give young people access to adults in unique ways. Be sure that the adults do not become their own clique.
- Have adults sit with young people at meals, ride next to them on buses, and work side-by-side with them in preparing meals.
- Connect youth and adults as prayer partners for the event experience.
- Enlist the help of all adults with the chaperoning duties. Determine the specific duties of chaperones. Set behavior guidelines before leaving for the event; all participants—youth and adults—follow the same rules.
- Create opportunities for youth and adults to talk with each other, either one-on-one or in small groups. Encourage the adults to share their stories with the young people. Provide guidelines for adults on appropriate self-disclosure with young people.

Building Relationships Among Youth

Extended events give young people the opportunity to get to know one another, work side by side, manage disagreements, and have meaningful conversations. Here are a few things to keep in mind:

- Before leaving for an extended event, schedule time for youth to meet and get to know one another.

- Schedule a significant amount of time for community building at the beginning of an experience.
- Use songs, group puzzles, energizers, and community builders throughout an extended event to continue to engage all the participants. Singing a silly song together creates a sense of community.
- Mix young people into many different groups so they will have opportunities to get to know new people. When it is important for some programs to create small groups that remain consistent throughout the program, use mealtimes, social times, and other activities to provide for broader socialization.
- Allow free time in your schedule for young people to have unstructured small-group or one-on-one conversations.

Leadership Opportunities and Service

Young people who are spending extended time with one another have unique opportunities to provide leadership within the community. They also should be invited into service for the good of all the participants. This helps community to grow and young people to develop skills and Christian characteristics. The following ideas allow for such leadership:

- Encourage young people to serve their peers. Some events create more service opportunities than others. On camping trips let young people cook meals or tend the campfire. On retreats youth can clear tables after meals. At a conference they might need to make sure they are each responsible for meeting at a designated spot at the right time.
- Allow young people maximum opportunities to be involved in planning an extended event.
- Create leadership roles within the event—young people can lead prayer, present witness talks, lead community builders, and serve as small-group facilitators. Provide the training and support they need to succeed.
- Consider the suggestions and ideas of young people for handling unexpected crises (a flat tire or a fight between friends) or schedule changes; use their expertise.
- Provide the participants with the opportunity to negotiate around rules or new situations when appropriate. Help them learn to negotiate so that everyone is a winner in the final decision. Be flexible and open to a change of plans.

Faith Sharing

When young people have spent quality time with their peers and with trusted adults, the opportunity presents itself to talk about important faith issues, to share experiences of God, and to ask important questions that move faith forward. Take advantage of this!

- Talk about important faith issues—in cars, when sitting around fires, or when discussing service experiences. Do not forget the faith you all have in common, and be willing to ask the hard questions and to talk about God.
- When you are on a long car trip, it is often easy to talk about faith questions that young people have. Engage those in the car in talking about important issues, and use their experiences and thoughts to help answer each other's questions.
- Create opportunities for young people to talk in small groups about faith issues.

Miscellaneous Ideas

Here are some additional ideas to think about when managing extended events:

- It is natural for young people to find someone attractive and interesting and to have the desire to become a couple. When pairing off does occur, address the issue directly with the couple. Let them know that you hope they continue to get to know each other in the context of the group experience, but that exclusive relationships are not part of the event.
- Give young people opportunities to check in with those at home, but limit that access. It is hard to build community at an event when the participants spend a great deal of time talking by phone to friends and family back home.
- Manage the grief that sometimes surfaces when events are coming to a close. Provide a prayerful celebration at the end of the event, in which the young people can speak about their sadness that the event is coming to a close. Focus them on returning home with great memories, experiences, and stories to share with others.
- Ensure that young people know how to stay in touch with new friends. Provide rosters at events, or allow time for trading e-mail addresses.

18 Atmosphere, Attitude, and Actions

Environment, Atmosphere, and Attitude

Some environments are more youth friendly than others. Parishes may not have a youth room within the parish property, but that does not mean that a youth-friendly space is unattainable or that creating an appropriate environment is beyond the ability of ministry leaders.

- **Create a youth-friendly space.** If your parish does have a youth room, ask the young people for their advice (and help) on decorating it and deciding what is needed. If a space isn't specifically set aside for young people at the parish, ask the parish leadership if one of the meeting spaces can be set up less formally, for use by the young people and other parish groups.
- **Pay attention to room setup.** If twenty people regularly attend a gathering, do not use a room that seats one hundred. A large room can communicate emptiness. You will want to set up the space to reflect the activities implemented during your time together. If conversation is a key element, set up the components of the room in a circle. If small-group work is important, make sure tables or circles of chairs are ready to go.
- **Decorate with sight and sound.** A dull, silent room is not an inviting space for anyone. Try to look at a meeting space through the eyes of the participants, and then change it to be more attentive to their style and needs.
- **Use music and video resources.** The use of music and video resources creates a comfortable and familiar environment for young people. When trying to teach a lesson, to make a point, or simply to entertain, music, movies, music videos, and television are valuable tools.
- **Provide a place for play.** Young people are used to interacting through games and sports. Consider putting up a basketball hoop in the church parking lot, adding a pool table, board games, and art supplies to a youth room, or scheduling time in the parish gym for play. This time and space for informal play provides young people with a feeling of welcome.

- **Be attentive to attitude.** Young people are extremely intuitive and perceptive—they can spot a phony a mile away. They know when adults are really enjoying their time with youth and when they are just putting in time with them. By being attentive to our attitude, adults let young people know they are valued in the parish community and in the youth ministry program.
- **Ask, "What aren't we saying or doing?"** Missed opportunities communicate as much as those times when we say or do the right thing. If the only adults who speak to youth or address their concerns are youth ministry leaders, the young people will believe that those are the only adults who care about them. Helping the entire parish to acknowledge, celebrate, talk with, and smile at young people will make a huge difference in creating a welcoming atmosphere for youth in the parish.

Using Technology

There are many ways to connect with young people through the Internet and e-mail. Here are some suggestions:

- **Provide information.** Minimally, put the youth ministry calendar, necessary program information, and parental permission and health forms on a parish or youth ministry Web page.
- **E-mail rosters.** Young people use e-mail and instant messaging all the time. When young people participate in parish activities—especially when they participate in events where people have gathered from throughout the community, the diocese, or a larger area—provide rosters with e-mail addresses, phone numbers, and mailing addresses. Young people stay in touch and build relationships through the use of e-mail and instant messaging. Include adult participants on the rosters if they wish.
- **Send thought-provoking e-mails.** Once you have created an e-mail list, it is easy to send out daily or weekly reminders, or to target young people with information about specific current events. Consider sending out Scripture reflections, interesting questions, funny stories, insights into current events, and other things that will get young people talking with one another. Let them use the information you provide to start a faith-based conversation at the school lunch table, in the car with friends, or at the family dinner table.
- **Publicize events.** Use your e-mail list and Web page to publicize youth ministry, community, and parish events.
- **Create virtual communities.** If your parish has access to technology that makes it possible to host chat groups, schedule chat times during the week (especially late at night) when young people can talk with one another about current events, faith issues, and community needs. Enlist

an adult to be part of the conversation, answer questions, and ensure that the conversation stays appropriate.

- **Provide links to good Web sites.** Connect your Web page to good local or national Web sites. For example, the Disciples Now Web site, *www.disciplesnow.com,* gives young people an opportunity to talk with other Catholic youth throughout the country. You will need written permission to link your Web page to other Web sites. Contact the Webmaster for each site to ask for permission.

Program Designs and Hints

Every program, event, or conversation has the potential for helping a young person feel comfortable and valued. By paying attention to community-life issues in the programs you select and provide, you can help the community that is built within your parish youth ministry program.

- **Be attentive to new people.** Every group faces the problem of becoming a clique when the same people attend on a regular basis. When new people come to a program or event, make sure that everyone reaches out to them and welcomes them into the community.
- **Encourage interaction.** When young people arrive at an event, they should be greeted and engaged in conversation or an activity. By being attentive to hospitality, the participants will not experience that awkward time of discomfort or uneasiness that they often feel when they are new or just getting to know people. Play a common game, start a conversation, or ask for help with setup; this gives young people a safe way of interacting.
- **Spend the time to build community.** Adults often are so interested in getting to the information or the program activities—which they believe are most important—that they ignore the importance of building community. We can't expect young people to share personal faith stories if they don't know one another's names. The times used to build community and create trusting relationships within the group is time well spent.
- **Define the role of competition.** No matter what the activity may be, consider the amount and style of competition that is involved. Are all recreation times or icebreakers built around competition? Are activities designed around who can complete the project first? Competition isn't always bad, but too much of it can create an atmosphere in which young people don't know how to act other than in competition with each other.
- **Choose fund-raisers that build community.** Many parishes spend a significant amount of time raising money. When choosing fund-raisers, consider how each fund-raiser contributes to building community, both among the young people and between the young people and the parish community. Fund-raisers that involve individuals selling to neighbors do

little to build community, but a car wash can be a fun experience for the young people and a benefit for the community.
- **Provide community meals.** Many parishes gather young people for dinner before an evening event, and ask families to provide and prepare the dinner. This provides an opportunity for large-group community building, and can be especially valuable before religious education or other programs where young people will be divided into smaller groups for the majority of the scheduled time.
- **Create social times.** By being attentive to the way you schedule events, most programs can include time for social interaction. By providing a little food, a space for recreation, and opportunities for small-group conversations, young people can have a safe place to find out more about one another, talk about things that interest them, and discover common interests.

19 Helping Families Connect

Overview

Given the changes that take place in adolescence, youth need the anchor of family, a sense of belonging, and the feeling of being at home, more than ever before. Family connectedness with adolescents is different from the connectedness that a family with younger children experiences.

During adolescence a young person's interests change, and their sense of independence grows. They are in transition, and their relationships with family members will change. The way of being family needs to grow and change with this new reality. This is difficult for both the parents and the young person, as each try to find their new place in the parent-child relationship. While young people try to assert their independence, make their own decisions, and live with the consequences, they still need the love and support of their parents. Parents have the difficult job of trying to figure out how to give their children just the right amount of independence mixed with the appropriate amount of direction. Parents are expected to be patient with their children through all the adolescent mood swings and declarations of "you're not fair," and find ways to express love that are not smothering. It is not an easy job!

The following strategies are taken from the real-life files of parents who are raising adolescents. Those parents have found strategies that work for them. Perhaps they will work for the parents of your community, or help them think of an idea that will work in their situation. These strategies are shared as a reproducible resource that can be distributed to parents through the parish bulletin, on a Web site, or as a handout for a parents' meeting. Additionally, you could provide parents with the ideas listed on the resource, one at a time, through a weekly "family ideas" section in a parish bulletin or on a Web site. Although the ideas are specifically written with teenagers in mind, many of them may be used with children of all ages.

Raising Adolescents

Families are a system—and anytime something changes in one part of the system, the whole system is affected. As young people develop through adolescence, all the changes that accompany such development will have a profound effect on the family as a whole. However, that effect need not be negative. Healthy families can embrace young people through this transition, providing them with appropriate levels of support and care within the family system, while at the same time giving them the independence necessary for continued growth.

Along with a growing sense of independence, your teenager's interests are also growing and changing. Your teenager is in transition, and all existing relationships will be different. The way of "being family" needs to grow with this new reality. It is difficult at best for you as a parent and for your son or daughter to find your new places in the parent-child relationship and in your family system as a whole. Although your son or daughter is trying to assert independence, make his or her own decisions, and live with the consequences, it does not mean that your child does not want your love and support. It may just mean that your adolescent doesn't always know how to ask for it, and that you don't always know how to give it in new ways.

Guiding Principles

Listed in the following section are ideas you can use to keep your family connected during the adolescent years. You are the best person to decide what will work for you and your family. Following are a few principles to keep in mind to guide your choices:

- Find new ways to be together as a family, because as your children get older, they will need to find new ways of relating to you as parents and to younger or older siblings.
- Take advantage of one-on-one time with your adolescent, and be available for conversations.
- Learn about your children's interests, support their new endeavors, and give them the freedom to grow and develop away from you.
- Share your interests with your children, and allow them to share in your life more fully.

Family Ideas

Make the most of the important days, and create some uniquely special days to let your children know that they are important to you and that spending time together as a family can be fun.

- **Plan birthday dinners.** Allow your child to choose the food or the restaurant. The other family members should work together to create the birthday meal or celebration.
- **Start a rainy-day fund.** Each day collect spare change from all family members, and periodically do something special with that money.
- **Do something different together.** Rent canoes and go on a picnic, go cross-country skiing even if no one knows how, try to cook a gourmet meal together, or cut down your own Christmas tree.
- **Create a family photo album or scrapbook.** Give all members of the family an opportunity once each season to capture the major moments of their life. Do the scrapbook together, or have each member do their page separately, and then have everyone talk about what they put on their page and why.

- **Have dinner together at least once a week.** Make food that everyone enjoys. Talk about the best and the worst events of the week. If dinner is not possible, create another time when the whole family can gather—for breakfast, a late-night snack, or dessert.
- **Make Sunday dinner special.** Sit at the dining-room table or use a tablecloth and candles. Have a dinner that is good enough for company; show your children that they are worth the effort.
- **As a family, commit to doing community service together.** Schedule community service once or twice a year at a time when everyone is available. The family gains a sense of pride in working together, and good family conversations about the experience take place in the weeks to come.
- **Create a "You Are Special" plate.** Use it to recognize something going on in the life of your children. Use it the day they get their acceptance letter to the college of their choice, the day of a hard test, the day they get asked to the prom, or at other times throughout the year to remind all the members of the family that something important is going on in someone's life.
- **Take a mystery trip to someplace fun.** Take a trip, but keep the destination a mystery. Tell your children what to wear, but let them keep guessing what the activity will be.
- **Have a dinner theme night.** The kids create the theme for the meal and help prepare the food. If your daughter or son is studying a foreign language, she or he may have access to recipes and favorite foods that are not normally served at your house.

One-on-One Time

Making some one-on-one time with your teenager can help you both appreciate the relationship you share and create some new memories. Here are a few ideas to consider:

- **Discover shared interests.** Find something that you and your child enjoy doing, and make it a priority in the family schedule. Work on cars, go skiing, collect comic books or baseball cards, watch movies, play basketball in the backyard, make a quilt, bake bread, or shop. It does not matter what the activity is, just find a way to make sure that a month does not pass without spending time together doing something that you both enjoy.
- **Watch television together.** With multiple televisions in many homes, it can happen that families never watch a show together or have the opportunity to talk about what everyone is viewing. Commit to watching one show a week that interests your child, and make sure your teenager agrees to watch something you choose. Take the opportunity to discuss, not just judge, the shows.
- **Turn the television off.** Spend one day (or evening) with no television or computer or video games. Find other activities to do together: play board games, build a fire, tell stories, work on a house project together, bake cookies, or take a walk or a bike ride.
- **Take your daughter or son on a date.** Invite him or her to breakfast or out for an ice cream sundae. Create a time that is just for the two of you. Use vacation time for some one-on-one time with each child.
- **Use time in the car for conversation.** Keep the radio off, don't let Walkmans be used, and set the precedent that car time is when the family talks about the day, upcoming events, interests, family problems, and other light or difficult conversations.

Specifically for Younger Adolescents

Younger adolescents need your love and guidance as they begin the journey into adulthood. The way you attend to your child during this time will set the stage for your future relationship.

- **Play board games or sports with your child.** Young adolescents begin seeking independence from their parents, and there is nothing like finally beating your dad at backyard basketball or taking your mom's pennies while playing cards.
- **Attend your son or daughter's events.** Create some time afterward for celebrations. Take the whole soccer team out for pizza, or the family out for ice cream after the piano recital.
- **Arrange for a birthday card extravaganza.** Most middle-school students get few cards in the mail. Ask your friends, neighbors, and relatives to help you celebrate your child's birthday by having people near and far send birthday greetings.
- **Honor the age differences in your family.** If your child is the first to reach adolescence (and you have younger children around who get lots of attention), create some time just for the older children. Hire a baby-sitter for the younger children so you can do something with the older child or children.

Specifically for Older Adolescents

Continuing to build a strong relationship with older adolescents demands some creative ways of connecting with busy teenagers, but communicating your love and guidance during this time is essential.

- **Surprise your teen during stressful times.** Help them manage the stress of college applications, jobs, homework, and other responsibilities by occasionally leaving them a special treat in their backpack, volunteering to run an errand, or taking them out to a coffeehouse for an hour.
- **Make college visits an adventure.** Many teenagers arrive at a college campus anxious to explore real college life—so help them do just that. Walk through the areas that have fun shops, restaurants, and bars. Talk about the things you know they will enjoy about the area, and give them some friendly warnings (or personal stories) about the college bar scene.
- **Go out of your way to be present in their lives.** Even though many older teens have their own car or access to a family car, occasionally show up at work or practice just to say hi or to bring a special treat. Surprise them with a full tank of gas.
- **Ask your child to come with you to a special event.** Is your child interested in the performing arts? Has she or he shown interest in community-service work? When possible, do something completely out of the ordinary. It will teach your child some of the social skills he or she will need in the near future.

Acknowledgments

The scriptural quotations contained herein are from the New Revised Standard Version of the Bible, Catholic Edition. Copyright © 1993 and 1989 by the Division of Christian Education of the National Council of the Churches of Christ in the United States of America. All rights reserved.

The material labeled *CYB* or *The Catholic Youth Bible* is from *The Catholic Youth Bible,* first edition (Winona, MN: Saint Mary's Press, 2000). Copyright © 2000 by Saint Mary's Press. All rights reserved.

The information about the goals and vision for ministry with adolescents on pages 7–8, and the excerpts on pages 21, 22, 22, 156, and 157 are from *Renewing the Vision: A Framework for Catholic Youth Ministry,* by the United States Conference of Catholic Bishops' (USCCB) Department of Education (Washington, DC: USCCB, 1997), pages 1–2, 34, 13, 34, 22, and 13, respectively. Copyright © 1997 by the USCCB, Inc. All rights reserved. Used with permission.

The information on pages 21–22 is from "Effective Youth Ministry Practices in Catholic Parishes," a joint research project of the Center for Ministry Development and Saint Mary's Press. The study is being published in *Effective Practices for Dynamic Youth Ministry* (Winona, MN: Saint Mary's Press, forthcoming).

The excerpt on page 23 is from *Grading Grown-Ups 2002: How Do American Kids and Adults Relate?,* a national study by Search Institute with support from Thrivent Financial for Lutherans, page 5.

The prayer on page 24 is from *Finding the Calm: Biblical Meditations to Nourish Those Who Nurture Teens,* by David Haas (Winona, MN: Saint Mary's Press, 2003), page 39. Copyright © 2003 by David Haas. All rights reserved. Used with permission.

The activity on pages 41–42 is adapted from *Jumpstarters: 100 Games to Spark Discussions* (Loveland, CO: Group Publishing, 2001), page 10. Copyright © 2001 by Group Publishing. All rights reserved. Used with permission.

Resource 1 is taken from Don Lowry's *True Colors* (Riverside, CA: Communication Companies, International). All rights reserved. Used with permission.

The excerpt "Our Deepest Fear," on resource 2, is from *A Return to Love: Reflections on the Principles of "A Course in Miracles,"* by Marianne Williamson [New York: Harper Collins, 1992], chapter 7, section 3, at *www.skdesigns.com/internet/articles/quotes/williamson.html,* accessed May 6, 2003.

The excerpt by John Donne on page 54 is from *Devotions Upon Emergent Occasions,* Meditation XVII, at *garnet.indstate.edu/ilnprof/ENG451/ISLAND/island1.html,* accessed May 30, 2003.

The excerpts on page 57 and resource 7 are from *The Holy Longing: The Search for a Christian Spirituality,* by Ronald Rolheiser (New York: Doubleday, 1999), pages 79–80 and 166. Copyright © 1999 by Ronald Rolheiser.

The excerpts from *Sons and Daughters of the Light* on handout 2 are from *Sons and Daughters of the Light: A Pastoral Plan for Ministry with Young Adults,* by the USCCB (Washington, DC: USCCB, 1997), page 19. Copyright © 1996 by the USCCB. All rights reserved. Found at *www.usccb.org/laity/ygadult/toc.htm,* accessed May 30, 2003.

The excerpt from *Economic Justice for All* on handout 2 is from *Economic Justice for All: Pastoral Letter on Catholic Social Teaching and the U.S. Economy,* by the USCCB (Washington, DC: USCCB, 1986), numbers 86–87. Copyright © 1986 by the USCCB. All rights reserved. Found at *www.osjspm.org/cst/eja.htm,* accessed May 30, 2003.

The excerpt from the *Decree on the Apostolate of the Laity* on handout 2 is from Vatican Council II, *Decree on the Apostolate of the Laity,* 1965, number 3, at *www.vatican.va/archive/hist_councils/ii_vatican_council/documents/vat-ii_decree_19651118_apostolicam-actuositatem_en.html,* accessed May 14, 2003.

The excerpt from *On the Permanent Validity of the Church's Missionary Mandate* on handout 2 is from John Paul II, *On the Permanent Validity of the Church's Missionary Mandate,* 1990, number 15, at *www.vatican.va/holy_father/john_paul_ii/ encyclicals/documents/hf_jp-ii_enc_07121990_redemptoris-missio_en.html,* accessed May 14, 2003.

The excerpt from *Dogmatic Constitution on the Church* on handout 2 is from Vatican Council II, *Dogmatic Constitution on the Church [Lumen Gentium],* 1964, number 33, at *www.vatican.va/archive/hist_councils/ii_vatican_council/documents/ vat-ii_const_19641121_lumen-gentium_en.html,* accessed May 14, 2003.

The excerpts on pages 66 and 81 are from the articles "Jesus' Imperfect Friends" near Matthew 26:36–45 and "Psalm 150, Part 2" near Psalm 150, the reflection on page 89 is adapted from the article "A Spiritual Checkup," near 2 Corinthians, chapter 13, and the reflection on page 103 is adapted from the article "Do You Trust Jesus?" near Matthew 14:22–33, in *The Catholic Youth Bible,* first edition (Winona, MN: Saint Mary's Press, 2000). Copyright © 2000 by Saint Mary's Press. All rights reserved.

The human rights listed on handout 5 are adapted from the Vatican Council II document *Pastoral Constitution on the Church in the Modern World [Gaudium et Spes],* 1965, number 26, at *www.vatican.va/archive/hist_councils/ii_vatican_council/ documents/vat-ii_cons_19651207_gaudium-et-spes_en.html,* accessed May 27, 2003.

The quotation on page 117 is from the song "Friends," in *The First Decade: 1983–1993,* by Michael W. Smith, writer Deborah D. Smith. Copyright © 1982 by Meadowgreen Music Company (ASCAP). International copyright secured. All rights reserved. Used with permission.

The prayers on page 136 and resource 8 are adapted from "Prayer for Religious Dialogue" and "Prayer for the Spread of Truth," in *Prayers of Blessing and Praise for All Occasions,* by Hugo Schlesinger and Humberto Porto (Mystic, CT: Twenty-Third Publications, 1987), pages 102–103 and 85. Copyright © 1987 by Hugo Schlesinger and Humberto Porto. Used with permission.

The five steps for community building and the excerpts and quotation on pages 141–143 are adapted from and quoted from *Building Community in Youth Groups,* by Denny Rydberg (Loveland, CO: Group Books, 1985), pages 18–21. Copyright © 1985 by Thom Schultz Publications. Used with permission.

To view copyright terms and conditions for Internet materials cited here, log on to the home pages for the referenced Web sites.

During the preparation of this manual and CD-ROM, all citations, facts, figures, names, addresses, telephone numbers, Internet URLs, and other information cited within were verified for accuracy. The authors and Saint Mary's Press staff have made every attempt to reference current and valid sources, but we cannot guarantee the content of any source, and we are not responsible for any changes that may have occurred since our verification. If you find an error in, or have a question or concern about, any of the information or sources listed within, please contact Saint Mary's Press.

Endnotes from *Economic Justice for All*

Chapter 4, handout 2

1. On the recent use of this term see: Congregation for the Doctrine of the Faith, "Instruction on Christian Freedom and Liberation," 46–50, 66–68; "Evangelization in Latin America's Present and Future," Final Document of the Third General Conference of the Latin American Episcopate (Puebla, Mexico, January 27–February 13, 1979), esp. part VI, ch. 1, "A Preferential Option for the Poor," in J. Eagleson and P. Scharper, eds, "Puebla and Beyond" (Maryknoll, NY: Orbis Books, 1979), 264–267; Donald Dorr, "Option for the Poor: A Hundred Years of Vatican Social Teaching" (Dublin: Gill and Macmillan/Maryknoll, NY: Orbis Books, 1983).
2. Octogesima Adveniens, 23.